SCOTTISH WRITERS SERIES

Editor

DAVID DAICHES

LEWIS GRASSIC GIBBON

by Ian Campbell

Ian Campbell has been interested in Lewis Grassic Gibbon since attending Mackie Academy in Stonehaven, and living in Inverbervie on the edge of Gibbon's Arbuthnott. He has had the good fortune to know not only several friends of the author, but also Mrs Mitchell, Rhea and Daryll who have been generous in providing both help and access to family papers. The present volume comes during a period of reviving interest in Gibbon's work with considerable critical attention, television serialisation, widespread study at School and University level, and long-overdue republication of work out of print (*The Thirteenth Disciple*, short stories) or work never before published (*The Speak of the Mearns*, 1982).

A Reader in English Literature at Edinburgh University, Ian Campbell specialises in the literature of the Victorian age (particularly Thomas Carlyle) and in Scottish literature since the Enlightenment. He recently edited a book of essays on Nineteenth Century Scottish fiction, and wrote a study of the Kailyard. He is Associate Editor of the Duke-Edinburgh edition of *The Collected Letters of Thomas and Jane Welsh Carlyle*.

LEWIS GRASSIC GIBBON

IAN CAMPBELL

SCOTTISH ACADEMIC PRESS

EDINBURGH

1985

Published by
Scottish Academic Press Ltd
33 Montgomery Street, Edinburgh EH7 5JX

First published 1985
SBN 7073 0365 6

© 1985 Ian Campbell

Printed in Great Britain by
Clark Constable, Edinburgh, London, Melbourne

ACKNOWLEDGMENTS

I owe a large debt to many who knew James Leslie Mitchell in life, above all to Ray, his wife and his most loyal supporter. To Ray, to her daughter Rhea and the other members of the family, my warmest thanks. In its earlier stages my interest, and this study, were stimulated by the kindness and help of Helen Cruickshank who was always keen to help Scottish literary studies, as she had helped Leslie Mitchell in his lifetime. Now that her papers, and the Mitchell papers, are in public hands the extent of our debt to both is more visible. My thanks to James Ritchie and Stanley Simpson in the National Library of Scotland, and to C. P. Finlayson and John Hall in Edinburgh University Library; my thanks, too, to Aberdeen University Library, Aberdeen Central Library, Stirling University Library, Montrose Public Library, the Mitchell Library in Glasgow, the Bodleian Library in Oxford and the British Library.

Gerald Bannerman of Inverbervie, who knew both Leslie Mitchell and the countryside of his books intimately, has been patiently helpful over many years. David Daiches guided the book to publication, and the writing of it was hastened by the help of many friends, particularly by David, Ruth and William Hutchison. Finally, my thanks for many things in this book to my father, whose parish bounded Kinraddie for many years.

Ian Campbell
Edinburgh, December 1983.

ABBREVIATIONS

Quotations are identified in the text by parenthetical attributions using the following code:

The Calends of Cairo	1934	CC
The Conquest of the Maya	1934	CM
Gay Hunter	1934	GH
Hanno	1928	H
Image and Superscription	1933	I&S
The Lost Trumpet	1932	LT
Niger	1934	N
Nine Against the Unknown	1934	NAU
A Scots Quair		
(Sunset Song	1932	
Cloud Howe	1933	
Grey Granite	1934	
published as a trilogy)	1946	S
Scottish Scene	1934	ScS
Spartacus	1935	Sp
The Speak of the Mearns	1982	SoM
Stained Radiance	1930	SR
The Thirteenth Disciple	1931	TD
Three Go Back	1932	TGB

The texts used are those of the first edition, except for the Hutchinson edition of the *Quair*, where the 15th impression of 1978 has been used. This modern, widely-available edition has the page numbers consecutively throughout from 1 to 496, replacing earlier impressions where the novels were paginated separately. The consecutive page numbering is shared with the hardback Schocken books reprint in the USA of 1979, though not with the Pocket Books paperback version which has been reset.

INTRODUCTION

James Leslie Mitchell (1901–35), Scottish novelist, has long been an enigma. The recent success of Lewis Grassic Gibbon, Mitchell's alias, is more easy to understand, particularly since the appearance on television first of *Sunset Song*, then of the short stories which translated so well into a new medium, and now of the complete trilogy. Paperback publication in Europe and North America as well as in Britain has brought him to public attention. Perhaps more remarkably, he has achieved a position of popularity in Scottish schools which is almost incredible to those who knew him only as a minor figure on the reading horizons of the early 1960s. Along with Neil Gunn, Lewis Grassic Gibbon stands unchallenged among the outstanding figures of modern Scottish fiction.

The enigmas remain. Mitchell the man sheltered behind the façade of Gibbon the novelist, indeed played games when he copied his close friend Chris Grieve (Hugh MacDiarmid) to quote himself, to attack himself, even to review himself under his alias. Again like Grieve, he invited easy encapsulation, yet produced a flood of material sufficiently diverse to make easy generalisation facile and ridiculous. A passionate Marxist of a closely defined nature, he was well aware of the limitations of his political creed; a passionate anti-Nationalist in a closely defined sense, he was one of the strongest forces to motivate nationalist movements in his time, and to give some focus to nationalist aspirations even today. A devotee of Arbuthnott, the Kinraddie of *Sunset Song*, he lost no opportunity to paint up its seamier side, and shrank from visits back even to family and friends. A lover of the country, he lived from choice in a garden city and commuted to London frequently. A fierce individualist, he revelled in distinguished literary company both in London and in Scotland. Above all, an evolving intellect and a maturing talent in his mid-30s, he died on the edge of producing a literature which could have had a profound effect on the modern Scottish consciousness.

This study is hardly likely to resolve these contradictions and paint the whole man. It does, however, offer certain objectives in coming to terms with the many-sided genius of Mitchell/Gibbon. It will be convenient, from time to time, to refer to work published under either name, but it is as Gibbon that he has passed into the public mind, and as Gibbon that we will, after the biographical chapter, discuss him.

First, we must see briefly how he grew up at a time most likely to produce the conflicting emotions of his novels, particularly when he refers to his native country. Second, we must briefly separate from his considerable bulk of published work certain recurrent themes. Third, in discussing these themes we may offer a certain insight into his work. Fourth, we may attempt an overall assessment, in particular referring to a wider context than that created by his own highly original talent.

Other authors, particularly Douglas F. Young, have given the works of Gibbon novel-by-novel coverage, and a considerable quantity of unpublished material in thesis form continues this process. Within the limitations of length imposed by this series, it has seemed much more useful to give a broad conspectus based on themes which haunted Gibbon's creative imagination.

Inevitably, we will discuss *A Scots Quair* at length, for there the themes come together into a synthesis which is largely successful. The extraordinary popularity of the trilogy is due in part no doubt to its intrinsic merits of language, handling of character, and readable descriptions of rural Scotland early in the present century. In addition, we will argue that its success depends on its handling of recurrent themes not as ideas forced on a book, but as ideas which recur just because they are in the forefront of the author's mind, consciously or otherwise—and in *Sunset Song* they all reached the level of conscious expression more or less simultaneously, and effectively, in the compass of one short novel.

While it is pointless to speculate on the possible contributions of Gibbon to the Scottish novel had he lived as long as Gunn (a speculation which tempts the critic of George Douglas Brown no less than of Stevenson's Scottish fiction) it will be necessary to enquire as to the limitations of the techniques Gibbon evolves in *A Scots Quair* (the omnibus title for *Sunset Song, Cloud Howe* and *Grey Granite*) for handling the "Scottish" experience, or mind, or unconscious quality which is definitely part of his subject matter.

Finally, a brief survey of available criticism (too brief in Scottish literary history) will indicate what has been done so far, and perhaps suggest areas where research is actively in progress. Gibbon's recent success has not so far been accompanied by a flourish of definitive criticism. Nevertheless it has spurred readers to read, and publishers to publish. The process, which will take time, is too important to overlook.

CONTENTS

CHAPTER I

THE LIFE OF
JAMES LESLIE MITCHELL

Our subject was born, not in the Arbuthnott of *Sunset Song*, but in Aberdeenshire, at Hillhead of Segget, Auchterless, on 13 February 1901. Like Chris in *Sunset Song*, he was to move to the Mearns in his formative, impressionable years but he appears to have retained a close memory of Aberdeenshire. Chris's mother mentions Bennachie frequently, and at the end of *Grey Granite* Chris returned to Aberdeenshire (as her creator did, to write the closing pages of the novel) for the enigmatic closing scene. The very name of Segget is re-used for *Cloud Howe*.

James Mitchell, the novelist's father, was a farmer who shared some of John Guthrie's features from *Sunset Song*. He is remembered as reserved and taciturn, and he did not give his affections easily, least of all in public. His wife Lilias Grassic Gibbon—source of much in her son, but not least his pseudonym—is remembered much more as the person who did the public business, and was family manager. Her tribute, surely, is the affectionate picture in *The Speak of the Mearns*. She was forceful and her temper was respected—her bargaining was respected too by shopkeepers. Her hair was a fairish red, the colour probably that caught the attention of her son's wandering mind in Arbuthnott Kirk as he looked at the pictures on the stained glass,

> And the second quean was Hope and she was near as unco as Faith, but had right bonny hair, red hair, though maybe you'd call it auburn, and in the winter-time the light in the morning service could come

splashing through the yews in the kirkyard and into the wee hall through the red hair of Hope (S 20).

Husband and wife were at the head of a hard-working crofting family, with three sons of whom Leslie Mitchell was youngest. Their way of life was one of sternly repetitive work in a hard country, with few farm machines, few concessions to holidays or fun. Mitchell senior worked himself hard and expected no less of his family: Mitchell junior, already book-absorbed, hated the life and did his best to escape. There are frequent hints of this in the novels. Chris in *Sunset Song* is surely speaking for her creator when she responds to the snobbery of the teachers in Stonehaven who mock her accent or her origins:

> For the most of them were sons and daughters of poor bit crofters and fishers themselves, up with the gentry they felt safe and unfrightened, far from that woesome pit of brose and bree and sheetless beds in which they had been reared. So right condescending they were with Chris, daughter of a farmer of no account . . . (S 45)

Her own social aspirations are seen in terms of leaving the lifestyle of her youth, "getting her B.A. and then a school of her own . . . father and his glowering and girning forgotten, she'd have a brave house of her own and wear what she liked . . ." (S 57). Most memorably, he spoke for his parents' generation when he wrote in *Scottish Scene* of

> old, bent and wrinkled people who have mislaid so much of fun and hope and high endeavour in grey servitude to those rigs curling away, only half-inanimate, into the night. (ScS 294)

Malcom Maudslay of *The Thirteenth Disciple* also seems to record a moment from life, glimpsing the effects of his detested crofter background on his parents.

> His father's foolish face, tired and sagging to weariness in the upspringing flame-glow of a lighted lamp—

once, at such glimpse, he stared at his father appalled,
heartwrung. He had never known he was as tired as
that ... (TD 51)

James Leslie Mitchell's adolescence can be comprehended in terms of a convulsive rejection of this life. He is
remembered by school contemporaries as withdrawn and
aloof, reading in a corner of the playground with
indifference to boys' sports. Malcom Maudslay in *The
Thirteenth Disciple*, Chris in a different way in *Sunset Song*,
react to their environment by withdrawal, as did their
creator. Forced to work on the farm, he skimped the work
or simply rebelled. Mocked for his self-improving ways, he
responded with self-protective indifference interpreted as
pride. Chris is repeatedly characterised as withdrawn and
aloof; Maudslay, a less complex character, is shown in the
school train as seeking the company only of "his joyously
book-reading self".

His place sank steadily in every class; college
quarterly reports caused John Maudslay to goggle
uncomprehendingly. But Malcom, as indifferent to
the opinions of his teachers as he was forgetful of the
prowling carnivores of the examinations, squatted
under the Walls of the World, immersed in dreams of
their conquest. (TD 60)

The Thirteenth Disciple is a useful book for this purpose, for
its conflicting emotions about the author's native Scotland
are less skilfully disguised than in *Sunset Song*. Malcom's
father is as unhelpful and obstructive as possible:

'I've won a bursary', he said.
'What?' said Chapel o' Seddel, (TD 40)

in a cruel parody of the kailyard fixation with education
and "getting on". But the book is also probably fair in its
handling of the outcome of this confrontation: Malcom's
mother insists that the boy "get on" if he has it in him, and

Malcom, like his creator, is allowed access to secondary schooling when his labour on the farm would have been useful to the hard-pressed family finances.

It is difficult to be fair to these early years of the author, yet important to try. They are seen in his work through the distorting perspective of manhood in which a quite different social orientation had been achieved, in South-East England, in relative middle-class prosperity. From such a viewpoint the early Arbuthnott years must have indeed been hard to describe objectively. Yet there is little attempt at either whitewash or vilification. The stress induced in memory, as in immediate experience, by these years is turned to advantage in the creative process throughout from *Stained Radiance* to *The Speak of the Mearns*. Indeed these stresses produced some of the finest mature writing, particularly in those parts of *Sunset Song* which seem today to have retained their appeal.

Not everything in these early years was obstruction. His mother's wider vision ensured Mitchell's access to adequate education and books, fostered by the affectionate interest of a schoolmaster (Alexander Gray, who did much to preserve his protégé's memory) and the help of the parish minister who lent books. Alexander Gray recorded in the *People's Journal* (16 May 1964) that young Mitchell "read all the books in my personal library. He read all the minister's books. There was a big J. P. Coate's Library at the School. He read all its books also." Mr. Gray, admiringly, asked the lad where his brains came from— from his mother, was the reply. Certainly the minister of the parish who knew Mitchell in early manhood was struck by his intellectual energy and independence of mind, in testimony to the present writer. Mitchell, no lover of the Church of Scotland, still found pleasure in contact with its educated ministers.

Leaving this security for the wider world, Mitchell lost this good fortune. He simply walked out of the Mackie Academy in Stonehaven after a public quarrel with the schoolmaster, and outraged opinion in Arbuthnott, in Stonehaven, and with his employers in early journalistic work in Aberdeen and Glasgow by his radical left-wing politics, his refusal to join patriotic sentiments, his exaggerated adolescent independence of thought. He found his first stimulus far from his father's croft, in junior reporting in Aberdeen (joining the Aberdeen Soviet, briefly), learning enough Russian to interview the sailors in the harbour, travelling through the poorer parts of Glasgow to and from work in his second reporting job. Mitchell was closely observing life and modern urban society. He had grown up in rural society: from 1917 to 1919 he was to see Aberdeen in lean years, and from 1919 to see Glasgow. The latter was disastrous: he attempted to cheat his employers (*The Scottish Farmer*) of petty cash, and after his dismissal unsuccessfully to commit suicide. He returned to a family in Arbuthnott now convinced that farm work was the only way out for their disgraced son.

These unhappy years brought him something akin to the stored experience of his years in rural Kincardineshire. The anger which settles through the essays on "Glasgow" and "Aberdeen" in *Scottish Scene* has this source, as has the nightmare vision of poverty and urban squalor in Duncairn in *Grey Granite*.

Yet not even these experiences drove Mitchell back to crofting life. To escape, he did something so antagonistic to his lonely, introverted character as to suggest the intensity of his unwillingness to work on the land: he sank himself into the anonymity of the armed forces. From August 1919 to March 1923 he was in the Army, after which he tried civilian life for a few months. But the same reason as drove him to the Army—destitution—drove him back to the Forces, this time to the Air Force, from August 1923 to August 1929. They were in general years of tedium, repetitive routine, occasional intense dislike. A fastidious man, Mitchell disliked the closeness and occasional lack of hygiene forced on him by the circumstances of soldierhood.

An introvert used to writing, he needed silence and loneliness, and found them difficult to achieve. Yet the years in the armed forces kept him alive, and they allowed him two momentous developments towards a writing career.

One of these was the stimulus of travel. The Army took Mitchell to the Middle East, to Egypt and Mesopotamia, settings for his earliest written work. His horizons, already expanded vastly from the Mearns to the cities, now comprehended new civilisations, and his burgeoning interest in civilisation, social history, anthropology, archaeology were fired by the new sights and sounds. Against this were to be years of monotony in English bases doing minor clerical jobs, but the freshness of foreign travel (unattainable otherwise on his bare finances) never left his descriptions of the Middle East, and transferred itself to his descriptions of South America and Central America, gleaned as these were from books.

The other stimulus, more potent still, was his marriage in August 1925 to Rebecca (Ray) Middleton. The local boy who had escaped from the small town to the wider scene, returned for his bride to the girl who lived in the farm opposite. Ray Middleton, daughter of the man who was to become "Long Rob of the Mill" in *Sunset Song*, had grown up with Mitchell and learned to love and to detest the same features of their native area. They had kept in touch more or less steadily during the years of Mitchell's travels, and in 1925 they married to form a bond which sustained the author throughout the hectically brief writing career ahead.

There was no fantasy beauty about early married life, which brought loneliness for a forces wife, serious illness, uneasy early literary experiment and frequent rejection— and the spectre of poverty which still rankled in Ray's memory almost fifty years later. They were years of cheap lodgings and strict economy, dealings with city landlords and city customs with which both were unacquainted, cutting of corners and trimming of budgets. These years brought serious illness, but joy also: a daughter Rhea Sylvia, and soon after a permanent home, the newly-evolving Welwyn Garden City, to which the Mitchells moved late in 1931.

The story now moves with great speed. At the time of his move to Welwyn, Mitchell was an established author with a growing reputation as short-story writer, novelist, essayist, and amateur cultural historian. To this he added a reputation as science-fiction writer (with *Three Go Back*) and then, in the Summer of 1932, as a first-rank Scottish novelist with the publication of his great single success, *Sunset Song*. The book's reception was mixed, but clearly it was to be a long-term success, and Mitchell could turn to the business of writing to provide a steady income for his family—a son, Daryll, was soon to be added. Publishers were willing to entertain proposals, his writing went well, the trains took him easily to London to publishers, to friends, to the British Museum Library where he worked gathering evidence for his cultural history, filing the borrowing slips methodically so that his footsteps can be followed today. At home he built up an impressive library of contemporary literature and historical works. A succession of small but comfortable family homes in Welwyn were the bases in which he worked, alone, at top speed typing steadily a first draft which seems to have gone to a typist, then to the publishers with remarkably little alteration. Perhaps a version would be re-typed (and the first sheets re-used on the opposite side, at random, for another work—a nightmare for the literary historian who seeks to catalogue his manuscripts), perhaps Ray would read and comment, but mostly he worked fast, and alone. His output was remarkable, and must have seemed so even to those who did not realise that the two prolific authors James Leslie Mitchell and Lewis Grassic Gibbon were one and the same. Gibbon enjoyed quoting himself, his "distant cousin" Mitchell. Doubtless his publishers appreciated the speedy supply of professional, highly publishable material.

The Mitchells were a companionable family, and enjoyed receiving company and entertaining friends, both newly-made English friends, and older ones from Scotland. Their Welwyn home was happy and with success and recognition seemingly assured, James Leslie Mitchell was a relaxed and genial entertainer.

Visits to Scotland were more problematical. The same tension which remained in his mind—in the minds of both—from childhood experiences, inhibited an easy or natural return to their native countryside. Indeed one of Mitchell's finest pieces of writing, "The Land" from *Scottish Scene*, concerns itself centrally (most of all in the section "Autumn") with the dilemma of the returning Scot. For Mitchell haplessly had much the same welcome home to Arbuthnott as John Wilson had to Barbie in *The House with the Green Shutters*: little understood, his book often unread but condemned at second hand, and shied away from by those whom he had incorporated (often unkindly) in the pages of his narrative, he found little praise in his own countryside and, most wounding of all, in his family. Significantly, it was his mother's rejection which he remembered most: she complained he had made his parents "the speak of the place" through his insensitivity in writing of people and localities so exactly, and so unflatteringly, in *Sunset Song*. With little difficulty, places and people can be traced even now in the novel; but in the 1930s, with most of the characters still alive, it must have been far easier. Much was meant as a joke, some may have been the unconscious process of an author's memory, but it appears to have been resented on Arbuthnott's side, and their response resented on Mitchell's. His visits home were unhappy, his relations with his parents full of tension: he appears to have returned to Welwyn and his own environment, as it had become, with relief.

On 7 February 1935 the flurry of creative activity was

over. A gentle and thoughtful person, Mitchell had not made his increasing gastric problems known to others, nor allowed his doctors to be disturbed to examine him even when he experienced severe internal pain. When eventually he was hospitalised and operated on, it was too late to save his life. He died of peritonitis, leaving a wife and a young family. He left, too, a reputation which was just growing to its proper stature and literary Scotland realised that a major loss had taken place. The reaction in the press and among literary circles, including those in New York who had come to realise Mitchell's worth (he achieved publication in North America repeatedly, and was seriously considered for Book Club selection), was immediate and sincere.

Mitchell had, like his character Chris, long ceased to be a practising Christian and he was cremated without ceremony in London. His ashes lie in Arbuthnott Churchyard, in the shadow of the thirteenth-century Church which dominates his trilogy, along with his parents and his wife. When he was interred in 1935 there was a formidable gathering of Scottish writers and Helen Cruickshank composed her memorable "Spring in the Mearns": when Ray followed in 1978, there were present many Scottish writers, and forty years had begun to make some assessment of her husband's reputation possible.

Mitchell is described by those who knew him as of medium height and slim build, quick, practical—the impression remains of a physical similarity to D. H. Lawrence. He was infectiously and spontaneously friendly, to strangers on the road, to friends met in trains or on the street, to people in his own house. He felt moods deeply, including the loneliness of the writer, and relied heavily on the loyalty and support of Ray in the extraordinary pressure of his high-speed creative writing. He was keenly sensitive to his parents and his fellow-Scots, and felt their rejection with considerable bitterness. He enjoyed revisiting the places, if not the people, of his youth and researched the background to his Scottish novels with some care, even interviewing members of the clergy to try to make the details of *Cloud Howe* correct. He loved physical exercise, walking, climbing, cycling round the roads of his youth, climbing (like Chris) to the archaeological remains which still marked the countryside of his early years—though progress has done away with many of them including Blawearie's Loch and Standing Stones. He loved meeting friends from early years, talking, listening, storing up people and places to be incorporated in his fiction. He had a keen awareness of place and mood, and showed it devastatingly in short stories of the calibre of "Greenden" and "Clay".

Certain things Mitchell felt very strongly about. He detested cruelty, indeed was fascinated by it to an extent which almost goes out of balance in some places, such as in *Spartacus*. But it is not idle curiosity, rather part of a wider concern for humanity which suffered all around him.

> I am so horrified by all our dirty little cruelties and bestialities, that I would feel the lowest type of skunk if I didn't shout the horror of them from the housetops. Of course I shout too loudly ...

But even with this admission, anger is a strong motivation in *Grey Granite* and in *Stained Radiance*, and in the polemical *Scottish Scene* which he enjoyed sharing with Hugh MacDiarmid, even though each man wrote in ignorance of the other's contribution, and sent the material to the publishers quite independently. Mitchell felt for the common man: he was an open Marxist though a difficult one to equate with any of the existing political parties (a difficulty experienced by any student of MacDiarmid at this time too): his belief in the justice of the Marxist dream was matched by his detestation of the injustices of depression and exploitation, but his own creeds and those of his fictitious spokesmen fit few labels. His artistic imagination fixes on the details of starvation in Depression

Aberdeen, on the cruelty of Spartacist Italy, but it also fixes on the here-and-now of mental cruelty, the gossip of his native Scotland, the emotional starvation of a people reduced to the infinitely entertaining behaviour which is part of the appeal of his Mearns.

> ... One gossip would now meet in with another ... and they'd shake hands and waggle their heads and be at it, hammer and tongs, a twelve month's gossip, the Howe's reputation put in through a mangle and its face danced on when it came through the rollers ... (CH 52)

It is the people, as much as the Land, that are Scotland in Mitchell's work. Together, they form a passionate emotion in the author's mind, an emotion which focusses his fictitious involvement with his distant country. Mitchell never defined it more aptly than in his often-quoted description from *The Thirteenth Disciple*, challenging kailyard and twentieth-century back-to-the-lander with impartial ridicule. Life on the land, he remembers bitterly, is

> A grey, grey life. Dull and grey in its routine, Spring, Summer, Autumn, Winter, that life [of] ... servitude to seasons and soil and the tending of cattle. A beastly life. With memory of it and reading those Catholic writers who for some obscure reason champion the peasant and his state as the ideal state, Malcom is moved autobiographically to a sardonic mirth ... He is unprintably sceptical as to Mr Chesterton or his chelas ever having grubbed a livelihood from hungry acres of red clay, or regarding the land and its inhabitants with any other vision than an obese Victorian astigmatism ... (TD 23)

By *Scottish Scene* his mind had changed little—he even quoted the above passage from his "distant cousin", glossing it with further expressions of "bored disgust" at the "pseudo-literary romantics" who advocated a return to the land. "They are promising the New Scotland a purgatory that would decimate it. They are promising it narrowness and bitterness and heart-breaking toil in one of the most unkindly agricultural lands in the world." (ScS 295)

Clearly, there is contradiction here. The Mearns's most famous author expresses a view of the Mearns complex enough to have been the background to a successful novel about the Mearns, written from hindsight and with this disturbingly honest vision—yet retaining a view of the land sufficiently warm to ensure the book's success.

There, in the countryside, we find the first part of our author's literary vision. Certain themes occur again and again in Grassic Gibbon's work. We turn, inevitably as he did, to the real protagonist of *Sunset Song*—the Land.

CHAPTER II

THE LAND

The exploration of this theme is relatively easy, since Gibbon devoted one of his best essays to it. Yet what is most interesting about the essay is what it avoids. It avoids the temptation to revisit the scenes of youth, making agreeable if undemanding reflections on change and decay: like Edwin Muir in *Scottish Journey*, Lewis Grassic Gibbon made the exploration of remembered scenes the basis for quite painful and wideranging analysis. Equally, the essay avoids the temptation to mere debunking, which occasionally debases parts of *The House with the Green Shutters* to something like parody. "The Land" is part celebration, part polemic. It has the immediacy of remembered pain mixed with remembered pleasure. It is a landscape with figures where the attention begins with the landscape, then transfers itself to the figures.

> *That* is The Land out there, under the sleet, churned and pelted there in the dark, the long rigs upturning their clayey faces to the spear-onset of the sleet. That is The Land, a dim vision this night of laggard fences and long stretching rigs. And the voice of it—the true and unforgettable voice—you can hear even such a night as this as the dark comes down, the immemorial plaint of the peewit, flying lost. (ScS 293)

Yet even this sharp picture is only partial truth. "*That* is The Land—though not quite all. Those folk in the byre . . . they are The Land in as great a measure." Combine sharply-remembered physical sensation with the vivid apprehension of figures on this landscape, and the rich amalgam is the rural landscape evoked by Gibbon's novels.

There may seem very little new to this, particularly in the context of Hardy's success, yet in the shadow of the Kailyard there is definite progress made by Gibbon. Two themes do surface which are distinctively new, and distinctly valuable to the twentieth century exploration of Scotland in fiction.

The first of these is the dynamic tension between the immemorial life of the land as simply earth, and the changing patterns of civilisation which man imposes on that land. The second is the phenomenon of man as a product of the land, rather than of merely a social system.

It was clever to pattern the essay on "The Land" on the seasons, for (as he was to do in *Sunset Song*) Gibbon suggests a cyclical character, a possibility of change even through recurrence, even before he sets to the business of analysis in the essay itself. In winter he remembers the storms, the inert face of farming, the beasts stored indoors; in spring, the carting of the muck, the labour of the farmer in helping Nature's cycle. In summer the men come out into the open, their relation with their land visible and necessary as the work of the farm proceeds, and in autumn with harvest comes the climax of their work, and with it the climax of possible change—the coming of the machines, the disappearance of the forests cut down through wartime effort in the First World War.

This may seem intellectualised, and rightly so, for that is the author's approach to his material, bound up though it is with the emotional responses of childhood experience. The land is there to be described with immediacy, yet to be remembered with the hindsight of later analysis. Cycling past Drumtochty in summer, the author hears snipe singing, and gets off his bicycle.

> So doing I was aware of a sober fact: that indeed all this was a little disappointing. I would never

apprehend its full darkly colourful beauty until I had
got back to England, far from it, down in the smooth
pastures of Hertforshire some night I would remember it and itch to write of it. I would see it without the
unessentials—sweat and flies and that hideous
gimcrack castle, nestling . . . among the trees. I would
see it in simplicity then, even as I would see the people
of the land.

This perhaps is the real land; not those furrows that
haunt me as animate. This is the land, unstirred and
greatly untouched by men, unknowing ploughing or
crops or the coming of the scythe. Yet even those
hills were not always thus . . . (ScS 300)

Here it is appropriate to mention Gibbon's childhood
fascination with history and archaeology, a fascination
which haunts his characters like Maudslay growing up in
rural Scotland, which informs the science fiction pictures of
far future or distant past, and brings Spartacist civilisation
alive in accurate detail. The Ancient Civilisation of
Scotland haunted the hills which haunted Gibbon, and
stone circle and ruined building alike were significant to
the bookish boy who cycled round digging and exploring,
mapping out a territory of the mind which was to serve him
as a landscape for future fiction.

I had no great interest in the things around me, I
remember, the summer dawns that came flecked with
saffron over the ricks of my father's farm, the whisper
and pelt of the corn-heads, green turning to yellow in
the long fields that lay down in front of our front-door,
the rattle and creak of the shelvins of a passing box-
cart, the chirp and sardonic *Ay!* of the farming childe
who squatted unshaven, with twingling eyes, on the
forefront of the shelvin . . . but the ancient men
haunted those woods and hills for me, and do so still.
(ScS 301)

The land for Gibbon exists in a historical context. Apparently timeless, it carries a history of mankind buried in it, spread thinly on its surface which bears so lightly the marks of "civilisation". It is a theme made much of in *Gay Hunter*, where the eponymous heroine goes to the far future, and finds all traces of human civilisation pitifully eroded away by wind and weather. In scenes reminiscent of *The Time Machine*, she learns the lesson that Chris learned on the closing pages of *Sunset Song*, that the land endures, but the traces of civilisation soon pass. This is the first aspect of the land which any critic must note in looking at Gibbon's Scotland: it is real, vivid, memorable—but it is a dynamic view of the land, a land which exists in a context of human history, which comments silently on human characters passing over it. The tension achieved between these two contexts is of the variety and scale achieved by Lawrence in the opening pages of *The Rainbow*, or by Hardy at the close of *Tess of the d'Urbervilles*; the land itself, surprisingly little changed by humans, is available in its limited change as a commentary on the bringers of that change.

None of this is to deny the potent effect the land has on Gibbon, in memory or at the moment of encounter, to evoke emotional, unintellectualised response. Autumn, inevitably, is when he realises his Scottishness:

> Mellow it certainly is not: but it has the most unique of tangs, this season haunted by the laplaplap of peesie's wings, by great moons that come nowhere as in Scotland, unending moons when the harvesting carts plod through thickets of fir-shadow to the cornyards deep in glaur. (ScS 303)

This is the true Scotland, as much as the hated reminders of the wintery half-inanimate rigs: the fatness of the South-East, Gibbon readily admits, is as alien as the olive groves of Persia,

[so] interwoven with the fibre of my body and
personality is this land and its queer, scarce harvests,
its hours of reeking sunshine and stifling rain . . .

Loving and hating it, barred from it by choice and lifestyle
yet plainly living in it in creative imagination, Gibbon
makes of the land the half-living character in his books
which plainly he sees it in his essay.

And the living characteristics, we have seen, are
associated with human change deliberately contrasted to
the impersonal cycle of the land and seasons, or the
apparent changelessness of the land.

Gibbon's short stories have recently met with deserved
success, in republication (for school use) and in television
serialisation. Two of them, *Greenden* and *Clay*, well illustrate
the complexity of their author's view of the land. *Greenden* is
about city folk who come to live on a particularly isolated
farm in the Mearns, where the flighty and impressionable
wife insensitively cajoles, then forces, her weak-lunged
husband to work the hungry land day and night. All the
time it is she who is in love with the land, to the exclusion of
thoughtfulness for him. The strange love affair is plainly
unhealthy: the grocer buys Ellen Simpson's eggs which she
brings to her door,

> . . . and stand[s] still while he counted, a slow, canny
> childe; but once he raised his head and said: *Losh, but
> it's still!*
>
> And the two of them stood there and listened in that
> quiet, not a sound to be heard or a thing to be seen
> beyond the green cup that stood listening around.
> And Ellen Simpson smiled white and said *Yes, it is
> still—and I'll take two loaves and some tea now, please.* (ScS
> 74–5)

Inevitably, such an unhealthy preoccupation leads to
breakdown: ironically, Simpson gains a measure of
physical health and strength, while his wife breaks down

and commits suicide. The grocer is the man who discovers
the body, and knows that she is dead and beyond help,
"and the thought went with him as he drove through the
woods, up out of the Den, to the road that walked by the
sea and the green hills that stood to peer with quiet faces in
the blow of the wind from the sunset's place". (ScS 79)

Conversely, *Clay* concerns a man so passionately
devoted to his land (rather like Ewan to Blawearie early
in his marriage to Chris) that he neglects everything,
including wife and family, in what amounts to a passionate
emotional affair with his own farm. It really is grotesque,
yet the limitation and compression of the short story form
focusses the attention not on potential humour, but on the
horror of the wife's cancer unnoticed by an uncaring
husband. That the plot is plainly that of *The House with the
Green Shutters* in fact detracts nothing from the success of
this story, for its economy and skill are very noticeable.
Most of all, Gibbon brings the contest between love of
land, and love of people, into the open.

> . . . *Rob, I've still that queer pain in my breast. I've had it for
> long and I doubt that it's worse. We'll need to send for the
> doctor, I think.* Rob said *Eh?* and gleyed at her dull *Well,
> well, that's fine. I'll need to be stepping, I must put in a two-
> three hours the night on the weeds that are coming so thick in the
> swedes, it's fair pestered with the dirt, that poor bit of park.*
> Mrs Galt said *Rob, will you leave your parks, just for a
> minute, and consider me? I'm ill and I want a doctor at last.*
> (ScS 275)

The little details, after this confrontation, are all to the
point and very well selected, for nothing is to excess. He
returns from the doctor to the farm and to his work without
bothering to tell his wife the outcome: he is simply more
interested in his parks. When his wife dies, he meets the
funeral party in his working clothes—he had thought
hoeing the parks too important to be put off. When he, in
turn, lies on his deathbed his thoughts are not for himself,

nor for his daughter Rachel, but for his land.

> *You'll take on the land, you and some childe, I've a notion for that?* But she couldn't lie even to please him just then, she'd no fancy for either the land or a lad, she shook her head and Rob's gley grew dim.
>
> When the doctor came in he found Rob dead, with his face to the wall and the blinds down-drawn . . . (Scs 278)

And Rachel, left in possession, makes a very different decision from Chris in *Sunset Song*. Life, she concludes, is "just clay that awoke and strove to return again to its mother's breast". But definitely, she rejects this life-force from the land, the "power that woke once on this brae and was gone at last from the parks of Pittaulds" (ScS 279). The land is alive, and in the closing paragraph with no hint of over-writing (a common fault when trying to articulate this theory of the living land) Gibbon expresses most vividly his view of the Land in regard to living actors in the play:

> For she knew in that moment that no other would come to tend the ill rigs in the north wind's blow. This was finished and ended, a thing put by, and the whins and the broom creep down once again, and only the peesies wheep and be still when she'd gone to the life that was hers, that was different, and the earth turn sleeping, unquieted no longer, her hungry bairns in her hungry breast where sleep and death and the earth were one. (ScS 279)

Two short stories here unite satisfactorily the themes of the first part of our investigation: the land as changeless and changing, the temporary nature of imposed change, the shortcomings of our understanding of the land and its potential.

But what of the other proposed part of our investigation of the land? People, it was suggested, change too: they are a

product of the land as much as of society, and their change
can be measured against the land as much as against the
society which produced them.

Gibbon was very careful to spell out his relationship to
the land, as distinct from his relationship to the essential
urban constructs of a modern civilisation.

> I like to remember I am of peasant rearing and
> peasant stock. [I am] . . . conscious of an overweening
> pride that mine was thus and so, that the land was so
> closely and intimately mine (my mother used to hap
> me in a plaid at harvest-time and leave me in the lee of
> a stook while she harvested) that I feel of a strange and
> antique age in the company and converse of my adult
> peers . . . (ScS 293–4)

The result is the possibility of writing a picture of the land
refreshingly unsentimental: we are in the world of Gunn's
highland childhood, or Muir's Orkney: we are in a more
controlled version of Brown's Barbie, remembered with
dislike as the habitat of the "Scot malignant" rather than
as the rosy kailyard haven. Parody is possible in every
direction, of course, and parody is implicit in the
description of the author as peasant, even when he writes
from the suburban fastness of Welwyn Garden City. But
the whole essay is openly reflective: it analyses change (as
we have seen) from a safe distance, analysis of beauty
which meant nothing at the time in the Mearns, and has
come to mean something only at a safe geographical and
emotional distance.

Yet people change. In "Summer", Gibbon makes the
point that people on the land have not always been as they
are in postwar Scotland (a point heavily emphasised in the
whole of *A Scots Quair*) and people, as well as land, are
rapidly evolving new strategies for survival.

> They change reluctantly, the men and women of the
> little crofts and cotter houses; but slowly a quite new

orientation of outlook is taking place. There are fewer children now plodding through the black glaur of the wet summer storms to school, fewer in both farm and cottar house. The ancient, strange whirlimagig of the generations that enslaved the Scots peasantry for centuries is broken.

Part of the change is contraception: Gibbon sees in that the escape from large families, and divided inheritance at the death of the father, which had perpetuated the social order of the Scottish peasantry . . . Part, too, is mechanical advance responding to the needs of agriculture. Part is the sort of balance between farming and industry which fascinated his speculations in *Three Go Back* and *Gay Hunter*.

> Under these hills—so summer-hazed, so immobile and essentially unchanging of a hundred years hence I do not know what strange master of the cultivated lands will pass in what strange mechanical contrivance: but he will be outwith that ancient yoke, and I send him my love . . . (ScS 302-3)

And so change is possible. The peasant is not the immemorial figure on the cart chirping *Aye!* to the passer-by, but the figure in the short stories of *Scottish Scene*, capable of change, capable of responding to slackening social mores by taking on new responsibilities, meeting new ideas, if need be cutting old ties. *Smeddum* hinges on this very idea, with its portrayal of Meg Menzies, crofter wife whose "smeddum" or strength of character gets her through life's disadvantages, a large family, a poor farm, and a weakling drunkard of a husband. But Meg, the strength of the family (perhaps the author had his own mother partly in mind) carries on through everything, in what seems a conventional way, till deepening intimacy in the course of the story tells us more. Her husband may come home drunk, yet she protects his pride from his children's laughter, and "put him to bed, with an extra nip to keep off a chill": when he dies, "Meg Menzies weeping like a stricken horse, her eyes on the dead, quiet face of her man" (ScS 118–19) seems a contradiction of the tough, unemotional character we are introduced to earlier.

The sting in the end of this story comes when Meg, left to work her croft, does all the work of a man "through that year and into the next and so till the speak died down in the Howe" (ScS 120) and then survives ill fortune on ill fortune, her children running away and marrying in haste, till finally her most bold and outspoken daughter, Kath, runs away, works on an ocean liner, comes back to Stonehaven and settles as a grocer (never having married the man she ran away with), and disgraces all her family— save her mother, who seems now strangely unmoved, while she had fought like a cat for the sake of her other children's reputation. With Kath, somehow, she does not care. Finally Kath asks for money to emigrate with a man to Canada and live with him for a while, and to the family's vast surprise Meg Menzies consents.

> She's fit to be free and to make her own choice the same as myself and the same kind of choice. There was none of the rest of you fit to do that, you'd to marry or burn, so I married you quick. But Kath and me could afford to find out. It all depends if you've smeddum or not . . . I never married your father, you see . . . (ScS 127)

Which, given the time and the place, is a revolutionary viewpoint.

Smaller families, greater social mobility, more prosperity, all are allied in Gibbon's view of the land to the existence of strong characters, people who are willing to stand out from the crowd. The short stories in *Scottish Scene* depend on such people and so does the autobiographical content of a novel like *The Thirteenth Disciple*. Malcolm's mother is an interesting case: obviously a free-thinking and outspoken woman, she fails completely to answer her son's growing curiosity on such matters as sex. The only question he asks, in innocence,

> Her sallow face had flushed and her usual composure
> deserted her.
> 'You are a *dirrty* little beast'.
> That was all, in her slurred Argyllshire English.
> Malcom had started at her, hot-eyed, and blushed
> and stammered involvedly, aware of a disgusting *faux
> pas*. (TD 31)

The Minister in Malcom's parish who teaches the boy
simple archaeology, the dominie, the dominie's niece
Domina all help to release Malcom from such bondage,
yet the extraordinary country characters are already in
essence there, their limitations imposed by inherited ideas,
their freedom likely to come (like Malcom's) from travel,
increasing mobility and prosperity, the result of the
breaking down of the strange whirlimagig of the centuries.
In his very first book Gibbon pointed out that travel and
exploration were never more possible, their challenges
never greater.

> To explore an atom may be a greater achievement
> than to explore a continent, but actual *physical*
> exploration of the unknown—geographical, seleno-
> graphical, aerographical, stellographical—has a
> deeper and simpler urge and impulse. Far from
> having shrunken, its fields stretch infinite to the
> telescopic stars. (H 19)

The urge is the same which motivates the search for the
Lost Trumpet in one of his lesser novels, based in the
Middle East: the trumpet blows when individuals reach
self-knowledge, and the author makes it his credo that "I
believe it lies unblown in every troubled human heart"
(LT 286). Yet the Middle East setting of *The Lost Trumpet* is
a long way from the Mearns of the autobiographical
novels.

This has been a chapter on contradictions, on contradictory memories and responses. Perhaps Gibbon summed them up most cogently in his description in *Stained Radiance* of Thea Mayven's relation to the Scotland of her youth, the countryside she had left for a career in London.

> In Scotland, on the little farm where she had been born, she had hated the peasant life. In London she remembered it with gladness and with tears, a thing of sunrises and rains and evening scents and the lowing of lone herds across the wine-red moors. Yearly she went to Scotland for a holiday, seeking the sunset and peewit's cry. Then she would find her days obsessed with talk of cattle disease and the smells of uncleaned byres and earwigs crawling down her back when she lay in a field. She would long for London as her spiritual home and as a haven of security. She came back from her holiday and her heritage of the earth, homing to London like a lost bird.
>
> Then the old songs of the winds and skies of her grey northland would go whispering through her heart again ... (SR 17–18)

And Thea thinks of this while her husband John works in an RAF camp to earn money for their future home: the autobiographical content is very obvious, and the confusion of ideas attributed to character very easy to transfer to author.

Sufficient for the present to resume the section under review as a selection of divided responses and split loyalties. As a countryside of permanence, history and beauty Scotland obviously had a powerful hold on Gibbon: as countryside changing in his own lifetime, it obviously fascinated him and he hailed the change with relief for the sake of those who lived on it, as he regretted the change to something whose history held such attraction.

At the same time, the people who lived on the land fascinated him, and as his essays make plain, they constituted a significant part of "The Land" to him as much as the semi-living rigs or fields. The people, too, were subtly changing, and not only with the possibilities of mechanisation or resettlement in the factory towns; a new spirit was moving across the land, a spirit of freer ideas and the possibility of rebellion against the yoke of the centuries. It was an exciting time to be in Scotland, on the land, looking at it and writing of it.

Yet, paradoxically—totally credibly—Gibbon rejected absolutely the idea of living on it. Biographically, we have seen the tensions which made living in Arbuthnott difficult if not impossible. In "The Land" he stated his view of Scotland—for him, Scotland was the Mearns, so narrowly did he define the area about which he could write with conviction and the authority of experience. Yet before the publication of his major works, and still more after that, he could not be accepted back into his community.

Still more honestly, yet painfully, he saw another reason: he had changed, and the community he had grown up into had changed too. This is why his picture of the land contains the dynamic element, emphasising change in both appearance and settlement. The Kinraddie of *Sunset Song* is as much a casualty of these changes as the other Scottish *locales* for short stories and lesser novels. He could not go home again: there was no home, in that sense, to go to. Much too honest to pretend that change was not taking place (as the Kailyard temptation might have been) Gibbon put the admission of exile in the forefront of his art. His exile is from the comfort of a pastoral Scotland.

I am concerned so much more deeply with men and women, with their nights and days, the things they believe, the things that move them to pain and anger and the callous, idle cruelties that are yet undead . . .

Elsewhere, nights like this, up and down the great agricultural belts of Scotland, in and about the yards and the ricks, there is still some relic of the ancient fun at the last ingathering of the sheaves—still a genial

clowning and drinking and a staring at the moon, and
slow, steady childes swinging away to the bothies,
their hands deep down in their pouches, their boots
striking fire from the cobbles; still maids to wait their
lads in the lee of the new-built stacks . . . (ScS 305–6)

And this comes from the author who saw the strange
whirlimagig of the centuries broken, the Scottish peasantry
freed. It is a contradiction quite understandable in a man
who grew up with an emotional tie to such a life, and who
has escaped from it. Yet it remains for us, in Gibbon's finest
fiction, to see whether the contradiction will vitiate his
view of his country, or be turned to advantage. Unques-
tionably, the denial of such a tension would be artistically
fatal: the kailyard image of an unchanging, essentially
pastoral, unindustrialised Scotland would be the result. It
would be attractive, realistic, exportable, and quite false.
Gibbon's Mearns shares some of the qualities of Brown's
Barbie: it looks good, it sounds authentic, but on closer
experience it turns out to be an uncomfortable place to
live. This contradiction we will explore further in the
analysis of *A Scots Quair*.

For the present, we must proceed to Gibbon's second
obsessive theme, which in part accounts for the split in
personality between those peasants who accept, and those
who respond to change by themselves changing and
adapting, with smeddum. This theme is civilisation.

CHAPTER III

CIVILISATION

One of Gibbon's most adventurous books beyond his creative fiction was *The Conquest of the Maya*, the study of a civilisation alien to his European readers, and the conflict between that civilisation and that of the Spanish Conquistadores. Despite his mischievous hints that he had worked in South America Gibbon's knowledge was purely from books. And it was extensive, accurate knowledge which led to published lectures in specialised periodicals—and controversy with other scholars in the field over interpretations of both outline and detail. Civilisations had always held a strange interest for him, the vanished Pictish civilisation who left their standing stones among the Roman traces near Arbuthnott; the Egyptian and other Middle Eastern civilisations he explored with relish during his forces days. Gibbon wrote a piece of polemic into *The Conquest of the Maya*.

> For six thousand years the greater mass of the human race has dreamed and adventured in the mazes of civilization, and garnered intellectual wisdom and much of experience and belief and disbelief. But we are still the essential primitives. The sacrificers who ripped the hearts from the victims on the Tikal altars or the legionaries who drove the nails through the hands and feet of the Spartacist slaves by the Appian Way are not remote and freakish aliens, beasts and strange monsters normal to their day, doing normal acts, abnormalities we have passed beyond. They were merely, as we are, primitives enlightened,

> darkened, upraised or bedevilled by the codes and
> circumstances of a civilization ... (CM 149)

Primitives enlightened we may be, but the common
obsession to Gibbon (as to his fellow-Diffusionists) was
civilisation and its many forms, each of them sharing the
terrible potential to transform and debase the human
mind.

Diffusionism (treated at length by Douglas Young in his
critical introduction to Gibbon) is, briefly, a system of
thought and study which presupposes that all civilisation
took its origin from the upper Nile, where annual floods of
the river gave nomadic tribes the chance to settle, give up
their wandering freedom, and farm rich fertile plots. As a
consequence there rose the idea of property (farm land),
the need for defence (soldiery to keep off other nomads), a
social structure to control the defence forces (kings, nobles
and the rest) and finally a need for a structure to control
the social one—hence religion, the civilisation of the mind
which for Gibbon had an especial horror. It was all
artificial, and all unnecessary (to his point of view) and
thousands of years of civilisation had brought mankind no
further than the stinking slums of the cities, the sordid
history of class struggle and oppression through the ages,
and the horrors of the Depression years. Gibbon was not
alone, nor a far-out heretic, in his view, but part of a
widespread movement which shaded into others, including those who studied the civilisations of South America for
clues about the origins of our own (a movement far from
dead today), and those who sought in the legend of Lost
Atlantis something to guide them in understanding their
own modern Europe. It was a sincere belief, an outsider's
view in antidote to an uncritical acceptance of 1930s
Europe, 1930s Britain as the acme and best of all possible
worlds. From a land pillaged by War, to an army and air
force keeping uneasy peace, to the cities in the early
Depression, Gibbon had little reason to look on his society

as the best of all worlds. In Diffusionism, he found a body of thought which explained his society as the bankrupt end of a decaying and decayed system, exploitation and superstition about to give way to revolution and egalitarian freedom. Gibbon the Marxist and Gibbon the Diffusionist found themselves in hearty accord here.

The results of Diffusionism are to be seen most clearly in Gibbon's disappointingly neglected science fiction. In *Three Go Back*, the main characters cross the Atlantic in an airship, run into violent storms, and in the ensuing chaos find themselves shipwrecked when they collide with mysterious uncharted mountains over what should be the open Atlantic. The plot is simple and obvious—the island is Atlantis before its ruin, the time is the far past (the time transfer taking place during a violent electrical storm, a familiar device recently borrowed for a successful Hollywood film), and the predicament of the citizens of a twentieth-century civilisation stranded on an alien island is obvious. Gibbon's fascination with his own characters is in their response to a pre-civilisation environment, how they respond to essential freedom, freedom from class, and from clothes, from marriage and from social and political belief. The natives of this far Atlantis are people genuinely free, who have never known civilisation.

> They ran in silence, tall and naked, the sunshine glistening on golden bodies, their hair flying like the horses' manes. Golden and wonderful against the hill-crest they ran ... (TGB 99)

These, obviously romanticised, are the ancestors of "civilised" man, pointedly in contrast to the central character Clair Stranley, feeling the ennui of her rich civilised existence in London. "The mess of our lives! Civilization! Ragged automata or lopsided slitherers. Our filthy concealments and our filthy cacklings when the drapings slip aside!" (TGB 30)

Three Go Back includes a good deal of thinly-disguised

propaganda for the diffusionist viewpoint, disguised as introductions to a world before civilisation. In discussing nudism, for instance, "These people without religion are the most spiritual the world will ever see! They are quite unaware of their bodies . . ." (TGB 135).

> The veil, the priest, the wedding ring, the porno-graphic novel, and all the unclean drama of two beasts enchained by sex and law and custom were things beyond comprehension of the childlike minds in those golden heads or the vivid desires of those golden bodies. (TGB 142)

The contrast between the primitives, so-called, and the modern civilised man to whose world the characters are returned at the end of the plot, is very marked indeed: it is a contrast as indebted to the closing scenes of William Morris's *News from Nowhere*, as the general tone of the passages quoted above is to D. H. Lawrence in "A Propos of *Lady Chatterley's Lover*". Yet neither comparison really weakens Gibbon's case to be taken seriously: he copied Wells throughout his science fiction without reducing its artistic quality. Where the science fiction is occasionally to be faulted is its open tendency to preach. What it does is to suspend the normality of our "civilisation" in order to heighten the contrast between "normality" and the extremes—either in the past, before civilisation was developed, or in the far future, when civilisation as we know it has faded as far as it faded from the Eloi of *The Time Machine*. Such free spirits are the raw material of Gibbon's world, and such free spirits (people like Meg Menzies) are rarities indeed in a twentieth century twisted by a full inheritance of civilisation.

It is interesting to compare the science fiction hunters with the prosaic reality of the working classes whose world Gibbon shared—especially in the armed forces, where we know he found their company sometimes unpleasant. Garland in *Stained Radiance* joins the forces to survive in difficult economic times, and meal-times are not pleasant.

> Garland sat midway the length of a table. About him,
> hungry, simple, unwashed, the airmen ate. They
> talked as they ate, with full mouths and unscrubbed
> teeth. Their laughter was unwholesome and high,
> their appearance and demeanour truculent ... (SR
> 72–3)

There is more of the same, reminiscent of *The Road to Wigan Pier*, with the same cleanly man's anger at the oppression of the poor, mingled with distaste for the smell and the dirt which Orwell so exactly captured. We are back in the world of unsheeted beds haunting Chris Guthrie's teachers at school, the basic existence of Chapel o' Seddel in *The Thirteenth Disciple*, the irritations which spoil Thea Mayven's return to Scotland in *Stained Radiance*.

Yet this is more than the author in Welwyn cleaning his fingernails. There is real anger behind this description of a working-class reality which after all he knew in the forces, and experienced in dreary London lodgings, struggling for respectability with wife and young child on an always inadequate income—the very life Thea and Garland have to face in its misery in *Stained Radiance*. The anger boiled over in Gibbon's essay "Glasgow" in *Scottish Scene*, where Orwell-like he tried to shock his comfortable audience into an awareness of how the poor live.

"Glasgow" begins, naturally, in Loch Lomondside, the author preparing the audience for the coming assault by dwelling on the beauty of the country.

> This is the proper land and stance from which to look
> at Glasgow, to divest oneself of horror or shame or
> admiration or—very real—fear, and ask: Why? Why
> did men ever allow themselves to become enslaved to
> a thing so obscene and so foul when there was *this*
> awaiting them here—hills and the splendours of
> freedom and silence ... (ScS 137)

While in Glasgow—"In Glasgow there are over a hundred
and fifty thousand human beings living in such conditions
as the most bitterly pressed primitives in Tierra del Fuego
never visioned". Living five or six to a room, the room itself
in a tenement, such people endure a nightmare existence
which Gibbon treats exactly as Orwell treats Wigan, or
Paris, or the conditions of "How the Poor Die": he assumes
the average, well-intentioned, civilised reader simply to
have no experience of them.

> The hundred and fifty thousand eat and sleep and
> copulate and conceive and crawl into childhood in
> those waste jungles of stench and disease and
> hopelessness, sub-humans as definitely as the Mor-
> locks of Wells—and without even the consolation of
> feeding on their oppressors' flesh.
> ... And they live on food of the quality of offal, ill-
> cooked, ill-eaten with speedily-diseased teeth for the
> tending of which they can afford no fees; they work—
> if they have work—in factories or foundries or the
> roaring reek of the Docks toilsome and dreary and
> unimaginative hours—hour on hour, day on day,
> frittering away the tissues of their bodies and the
> spirit-stuff of their souls; they are workless—great
> numbers of them—doomed to long days of staring
> vacuity, of shoelessness, of shivering hidings in this
> and that mean runway when the landlords' agents
> come...
> ... Their voices are the voices of men and women
> robbed of manhood and womanhood (ScS 137–8)

We are in the countryside of Edwin Muir's *Poor Tom*, or
his *Scottish Journey*. And we have to be told: the investi-
gator, Gibbon's ironic term for the Scottish reader, is a
Kelvinsider, a comfortable civilised middle-class reader,
unaware of the grim realities for the majority.

This is powerful writing, not least for its assumptions

about those in Scotland who write novels, and those who read them. Just as Gibbon carried into his novels discussions of sex and marriage, to the distress of family and contemporaries in the Mearns, so he carried social questions to readers to whom much may have been novel. And behind it all was the obsession with civilisation. The nomadic hunters of *Three Go Back* knew nothing of the flush toilet nor electric light, nor indeed of marriage or of shame at their own nudity. No more did they know of tenements or the Docks, of unemployment or the Dole, of the external indignities of the poor, and the internal corrosion of their free spirits. Whether the poor are the soldiers whose lives offend Garland in their unhygenic details, or the poor of Glasgow whose memory obviously haunted Gibbon throughout his adult life, the over-riding concern is with the rescue of them from a cultural and social impasse.

There is a strong passage at the opening of Edwin Muir's *Scottish Journey* which underlines Gibbon's concern with the plight of the poor as going far beyond mere hunger —frittering away rather the spirit-stuff of their souls. Muir's inspiration for his travel book came not from Edinburgh or the Trossachs, but from Hamilton, Airdrie and Motherwell.

> It was a warm, overcast summer day; groups of idle, sullen-looking young men ... were wandering among the blue-black ranges of pit-dumps which in that region are the substitute for nature; the houses looked empty and unemployed like their tenants; and the road along which the car stumbled was pitted and rent, as if it had recently been under shell-fire. Everything had the look of a Sunday which had lasted for many years ... a disused, slovenly, everlasting Sunday. ...
> Airdrie and Motherwell are the most improbable places imaginable in which to be left with nothing to do; for only rough work could reconcile anyone to living in them. Yet a large population lives there in

idleness; for there is nowhere else to go, and little prospect that Monday will dawn for a long time.

This is exactly Gibbon's status as far as his attitude to the suspended animation of the poor is concerned. In his work his anger is directed not at the *laissez-faire* economics which allow the poor to starve, but at the ugliness perpetrated on the souls of the poor, at the system which perpetuates distances between the comfortable and the poor, and dignifies them with names like society, justice, religion, civilisation.

In Gibbon's writings, people build up defences against this encroaching evil. One of his early works was a biography of Mungo Park entitled *Niger*, and he mischievously depicts the Scottish background of his subject as "a code of suppression, of non-joy in the Sabbath, of the hearty eating of tiresome food, of conventionality of expression and demand" which most Scots accepted at the end of the eighteenth century, "but on Mungo, as on many another imaginative child, it fell like a stifling black blanket" (M 13). Stormont and Garland, two of his imaginative male characters, evolve a defence-mechanism in affecting a coolness, an indifference which protects them from emotional involvement which could be damaging in a modern city. Malcom Maudslay develops a total indifference to "the genial smut of the reporter's room" (TD 83) in order to cope with his civilisation's obsession with sex, when he himself has no fulfilment as a human being.

A difficult book to place in any context, *Spartacus* is worth noticing in the context of the present discussion. In it, almost no character achieves normal fulfilment: Spartacus is wedded to his rebellion (and never, formally, to the woman who bears his children), and his officers are likewise denied fulfilment by the pressures of their unjust society. Gershom ben Sanballat, the Jew, is misunderstood and only not mocked because he is feared; Crixus and

Castus, and Crassus are loyally discreet and of course Kleon the Greek is loyal to Spartacus because he is a eunuch, castrated by the Romans as an act of thoughtless cruelty to make a more docile slave of him.

In *Spartacus*, the real villains (the masters of Roman civilisation) are off-stage almost throughout. The foreground of the novel is occupied with those who suffer as a result of that civilisation: the slaves, the freed slaves, their women, their victims. Men and women robbed of normal home life, of affection, or any kind of fulfilment, are simply incapable of handling the limited freedom they achieve in their rebellion. Their loyalties are harnessed, if at all, to the crude and violent ideals of Spartacus' army. Spartacus' circle is notable for its unnatural restraint, its permanent nervous tension, its beautiful but senseless internal cohesion. They live together, fight together, and die hideously together in the mass crucifixions inflicted by the Romans on their captives at the end of the rebellion.

> And at length even the men of the legions turned in horror from looking back along the horizon at that stretch of undulating, crying figures fading down into the sun-haze. Some, nailed on the cross, shrieked aloud with agony as the nails scraped through their bones or splintered those bones so that ragged splinters hung from the flesh. Some fainted. Some cried on strange Gods, and now at last pleaded for mercy while the legionaries drove the nails home through hands and feet . . . (Sp 284)

It is a truly sickening scene, but it is civilisation; it is the return to "normal" values after the unnatural slave rebellion. Yet Gibbon paints "civilisation" in terms just as sickening; the world of Rome is glimpsed at a distance as one of pleasure and perversion, the world of the games and luxury sustained by a brutal system of the exploitation of slavery. Spartacus is exploited for his brawn by the Masters who wish to see him fight: Kleon for his brain by the Masters who want him clever—but impotent to harm the system. The historical rebellion is one ironical in the extreme to Kleon:

> And the Greek eunuch thought with a twisted mouth how the divine Plato would have stared in amaze had he heard it proposed that a Thracian savage, a slave eunuch and a courtesan hardly more than a girl should set to organizing the Republic which he had planned! Yet, ere the Romans gathered and ended the revolt for ever, the Gods might laugh at that jest ...
> (Sp 72)

Gibbon's view of civilisation would endorse Kleon's cynicism, and indeed he did not have to look much further than his own bookshelves, to J. B. Bury's *History of Greece*, from the library of the Central Education School in Cairo, doubtless a souvenir of his forces visit to the Middle East. The description of Euripides' attitudes to the establishment of his day is strikingly in anticipation of Gibbon's treatment of the Spartacist rebellion:

> He will receive nothing on authority; he declines to bow to the orthodox opinions of his respectable fellow-countrymen, on such matters as the institution of slavery, or the position of women in society. He refuses to endorse the inveterate prejudice which prevailed even at Athens in favour of noble birth ...
> (p. 389)

Gibbon's view of civilisation is not merely severe on ancient Rome: the civilisations which took over from the indigenous cultures of Central America attract special venom. Christopher Columbus, finding the first native humans on his new land, noted

> In fine, they took and gave all of whatever they had with good will. But it appeared to me they were a people very poor in everything. They went totally

naked, as naked as their mothers brought them into
the world. (NA 102)

Lacking even a creed, they satisfied Columbus' urge to see
them converted to Christianity, though Gibbon notes with
satisfaction that they had "the wildness and intractability
of the free wild animal", and would resist.

Resistance would surely be right: Vasco da Gama's
career of murder and exploitation in his settlement of the
Central Americas is recorded in *Nine Against the Unknown* in
sickening detail.

> Solemn mass was said, and the sins of the voyageurs
> commuted in invocation of that peaceful God whose
> name they were to spread abroad the Far East till the
> most obscenely cruel and treacherous of Easterners
> were to shudder with a sickened horror at mention
> of the Christians' God. Vasco da Gama had his
> company confessed and embarked. In the ship stores
> was a supply of oil, capable of being boiled and used
> for the questioning of recalcitrant natives ... (NA
> 172)

There is an uneasy moment here, the unspeakable physical
detail, recalling the obsessive concern with physical
cruelty, torture, mutilation which shows clearly in
Spartacus. "Of course I shout too loudly": Gibbon saw the
artistic fault in his violent protest against a civilisation of
which he wanted no part, but the violence of his feelings
made him unable to stop himself. Whether in reconstruct-
ing the violence of past centuries, or lambasting the social
evils of his own, or satirising the corruption of nature in its
purest form, "unstrewn with trippers' banana-skins,
unawakened by the music of the phonograph" (H 20) he
shared his schoolbook's attitude to Euripides, admiring the
iconoclast, being cool to the conformist, faithfully recon-
structing the wider picture while if possible slanting the
picture to highlight the rebellion against the uglier features
of civilisation.

One very obvious area of offence in writing in this way of civilisation is in Gibbon's treatment of religion. Like Stevenson he found this a bitter pill to swallow from his Scottish childhood and early on moved away from the conformist position of his family, in regard to Church-going, and then in regard to personal faith. In *Spartacus* he used Christ and the Crucifixion as part of the framework of a historical narrative rather than as an over-ruling symbol: Spartacus as rebel, and castrated Kleon as suffering martyr crucified on the Appian Way, are merged with the historical Christ more for the implied attitude to authority and rebellion, than for the consolation of Christian hope. The setting is Italy, the time not long before the Birth of Christ: the message is not one of Bethlehem but of Rome, not one of new life but of the assertion of the human will, briefly and hopelessly, against the encroaching might of a corrupt civilisation. The actual last words of the novel have more than a little ambiguity, reflecting their author's willingness to push into unknown territory and risk public offence. The words are in the mind of Kleon, dying nailed to a cross in an act of public sadism, already on the edge of hysteria after two days and nights of torture in the line of crucified slaves.

> And he saw before him, gigantic, filling the sky, a great Cross with a figure that was crowned with thorns; and behind it, sky-towering as well, gladius in hand, his hand on the edge of the morning behind that Cross, the figure of a Gladiator. And he saw that these Two were One, and the world yet theirs; and he went into unending night and left them that shining earth.
>
> *It was Springtime in Italy, a hundred years before the crucifixion of Christ* . . . (Sp 287)

In other words, a straightforward reading allows us to take Gibbon's point as being that Christ and Roman Slave are the same person, the historical Christ seen as Rebel rather than as divine Person. Which is potentially offensive to orthodoxy, particularly to the orthodoxy of Gibbon's childhood.

Against this, we must note that the cyclical view of history, though seen through the crazed mind of a tortured victim, is one which supposes eventual victory to the rebels. The world in this final vision belongs to Christ and Spartacus, even though Kleon's onward journey is to everlasting blackness. Theirs is another journey, one to continuing struggle and (it is implied) eventual success, in some undreamed-of future struggle.

Elsewhere Gibbon allows himself some hint of the eventual triumph of rebellion over civilisation, but he is still at best enigmatic. Nansen survives his polar expeditions to become a chained eagle in Norwegian nationalist politics,

> . . . to a long, puzzled neutrality during the War . . . to that ten year's spurt of energy in Russia and at Geneva which awoke for the world again the magic of the earth-conqueror's name—this time the conquest of pity and compassion, perhaps the truest conquest of all . . . (NAU 316)

His own personal anger at exploitation and injustice is part of his expression of that struggle. When he defended the Maya as

> . . . merely, as we are, primitives enlightened, darkened, upraised or bedevilled by the codes and circumstances of a civilization (CM 149)

he was expressing a dissatisfaction with working and upper class, with past and present, with internal dissension and public injustice which made him choose the Spartacist rebellion as the most natural of vehicles for expression. Spartacus, the climactic fight of his campaign ahead, stabs his famous white stallion to the heart. If he wins, there will be other stallions; if he loses (as he dimly must see ahead), the symbolic gesture is already made. It is splendid fiction, but it is not quite the position of the author. For the author, the protest against his time and his civilisation continues in all the acceptable forms of publishable expression, history as fact and fiction, novels of the past, present and future, essay, polemic.

The reader today who works through the novels produced in a hectic period of a few years in Welwyn is aware of repetitive themes, but also of repetitive characters. Protesters, nonconformists, coolly detached outsiders from their society fight to maintain their detachment against burning internal anger and felt involvement. They strike a balance, they find an acceptable self-expression, they find a way of life and limited happiness despite the urgency of their crusade. Above all, they find it not in conformity to the civilisation whose detested evidences surround them, but in human relationships which transcend the codes of that civilisation. The characters who haunt the pages of the Gibbon novels, whether published as Gibbon or Mitchell, have much in common with their creator. Caught between town and country, between past and present, between Scotland and England, he evoked the character of struggler again and again till he achieved the correct balance in Chris. *Stained Radiance*, subtitled "A Fictionist's Prelude", has much that makes it an obvious alternative draft for *Sunset Song*, and many of the problems recur in *The Thirteenth Disciple*. But Ray Mitchell must have understood the delicate *double entendre* in the dedication to her of *Stained Radiance*:

> Dedication of these Old Foes/ with New Faces to the laughter and pity of one/ who has known them in other/ guises: My wife,/ Rhea Mitchell.

The "other guises" are Scots and English, past and present, but they imply no poverty of creative imagination. Rather they imply a set of central ideas round which

Gibbon's political ideology and hostility to an exploiting society revolve. The boss and the worker, the landlord and the tenant, the minister and the parishioner, the worker and the leisured rich—these categories, alike hateful, are the categories which recur. The Gibbon narrative figures, like Mr Kipps and Mr Polly, share a bewildered apprehension of the injustices and cruelties of their society and their civilisation, but they perhaps more forcefully set out to do something about it. In the founding of political parties of the Left, in the expression of hostility to inherited prejudice and second-hand notions of political "right" and "wrong", the Gibbon characters show the possibility of continuing revolt. To some, it means loss of human warmth, in the straightforward sense of Ma Cleghorn in *Grey Granite*, Meg Menzies in *Smeddum*, Ma Anderson in *Image and Superscription*. These are the survivors, the working-class characters who simply get on with the business of rearing families and making ends meet, in cool (or heated) defiance of society's conventions and prohibitions.

Sometimes the anger is allowed a more intellectualised form: Gershom in *Image and Superscription* lives through the horror of life in the trenches in the First World War and sees at first hand the pressure on the uncomprehending working-classes of a sickening war waged by forces over which they have no control, waged for ideologies and political positions of which they know nothing, and care less. Gershom's friend Metaxa is crucified on the barbed wire of the trenches, and Gershom has to fire the bullet which puts his closest and most intimate friend out of his agony: it is a terrible moment and comes close to unhinging his mind, but it summarises splendidly for the reader the extent of Gibbon's passionate involvement with the cruelty which began the war, and sent out the human beings to fight it. The human attachment of Gershom to Metaxa, or to Ma Anderson and her pathetic husband Bill scalded and reduced to imbecility by an accident in the war, offsets the distant impersonal brutalities of the war exactly and artistically.

The two sides of civilisation simply do not make contact: one, suffering, survives with the workers of the world and scrapes by like the savages of all Gibbon's historical works, and the working classes of his novels of Britain in postwar depression: the other, rich and unattainable, is perhaps less immediately cruel than the Romans of the Spartacist rebellion, but their distance and indifference have as cruel effects, magnified by the strains of city living and the impersonality of it which allows injustice to be invisible and uncorrected—like Ma Anderson's care of her scalded and ruined Bill in *Image and Superscription*. So, in that novel, Gibbon comes completely out in the open:

> Civilisation and its superstitions, its blind follies ... a dream dreamt by a beast captured and tormented in a by-pass of Space and Time (I&S 245)

The alternatives are, as in *Spartacus*, more ambiguous than immediately available. Certainly religion is not the answer, as Gershom finds. "Religion, its terrors, its hopes and its hates were too remote from everyday life ever again to affect it greatly" (I&S 270). Nor, the style sometimes makes clear, does the over-intellectualised Communism of the clear-eyed idealists of Gibbon's own time, men like James Storman in *Stained Radiance*.

> His purpose was to produce money for the Anarcho-Communist Party. Pursuing this aim during the last two years, he had cajoled trade union leaders wheedled Socialist authors, begged from Moscow, borrowed from the French Communist party, and blackmailed business firms in Manchester. To the same end, he would have sold the bones in a London cemetery. (SR 54)

Storman, like Ewan junior in *A Scots Quair*, is an idealist whose commitment is perfectly intelligible without being admirable. Communism is obviously something Mitchell accepted as a just and possible answer to the exploitation and misery of the capitalist society he lived in, but the communists who put the creed into action, and their short-cuts in getting through layers of prejudice and mistrust, waken Gibbon's alarm and mistrust. It is a theme which will dominate any discussion of the end of *Grey Granite*.

Before that discussion, we must take Gibbon's obsessive interest in the land, and in political regeneration, one step further, to his third main recurrent theme—Scotland. The stage is then set for an extended discussion of *A Scots Quair*.

CHAPTER IV

SCOTLAND

"Few things cry so urgently for rewriting as does Scots history, in few aspects of her bastardized culture has Scotland been so ill-served as by her historians" (ScS 19). Happily, this trenchant opening to "The Antique Scene" in *Scottish Scene* is no longer so applicable as it was in 1934, but in addition to being a good journalistic opening to an arresting book of revaluations and re-interpretations of Scottish culture "The Antique Scene" is a good way into Gibbon's view of his own country. The authors of each contribution remind the audience in their "Curtain Raiser" that

> ... one wrote the most of his in a pleasant village near London, the other in the sound of the running seas by the Shetlands. They believed that distance from the Scottish Scene would lend them some clarity in viewing it. (ScS 11)

Gibbon's view of his country has sardonic bite that reinforces our first consideration of him—as an author of life on the land completely lacking in sentimentality. Scotland, remembered by Gibbon in this essay, is a welter of conflicting cultural and religious and political half-assimilated influences, in the age of a barbarisation which threatens to eclipse what little Scottishness is left.

> The Diffusionist school of historians holds that the state of Barbarism is no half-way house of a progressive people towards full and complete civilization: on the contrary, it marks a degeneration from an older civilization ... The state of Scotland since the

Union of the Crowns gives remarkable support to this view, though the savagery of large portions of the modern urbanized population had a fresh calamity—the Industrial Revolution—to father it. (ScS 32)

To explain his attitude, the author gives a brief Diffusionist history.

"All human civilizations originated in Ancient Egypt", and spread slowly through Europe to form the civilised world:

Before the planning of that architecture enslaved the minds of men, man was a free and happy and undiseased animal wandering the world in the Golden Age of the poets (and reality) from the Shetlands to Tierra del Fuego. (ScS 20)

Thus came the first settlements in Scotland, in Mitchell's view: settlements of Picts and Kelts, though Gibbon's scathing contempt for the Kelt is probably overemphasised in deliberate hostility to what he saw as the romanticised view of Scotland's history in the Gaelic revivals of his own time. "But if the Kelts were the first great curse of Scotland, the Norse were assuredly the second" (ScS 24). Norse, Scot and Angle form the hotchpotch of cultural inheritance from which recognisable modern Scotland is constructed: the Scots and English speeches developed in parallel, and Scotland briefly knew true independence of mind and art. Yet alongside this come the struggles of political intrigue inseparable from civilisation: the Wars of Independence ruined this early Scotland for Gibbon.

The effect of that war, the unceasing war of several centuries, was calamitous to the Scots civilization in the sense that it permanently impoverished it, leaving Scotland, but for a brief blink, always a poor country economically, and a blessing in that it set firmly in the Scots mind the knowledge of national homogeneity: Scotland was the home of true political nationalism

(once a liberating influence, not as now an inhibiting
one)—not the nationalism forced upon an unwilling
or indifferent people by the intrigues of kings and
courtesans, but the spontaneous uprising of an
awareness of blood-brotherhood and freedom-right.
(ScS 27)

Inevitably, Gibbon's hero is Wallace, who asserts this kind
of nationalism and pays for it with his life. He sets a tone, a
tone of individualism "in the succeeding centuries of wars
and raids, dynastic begettings and dynastic blood-
lettings" (ScS 29) which ensures the continuance of a
national spirit till the next disaster—religious reform.

That eclipse was inaugurated by the coming of the
tumultuous change in Christian ritualism and super-
stitious practice dignified by the name of Reformation. (ScS 30)

A Church "intellectually moribund" is forcibly changed,
in Gibbon's view not for idealistic reasons, but for political
hunger, for petty disagreement over ritual, and never for
the good of the country which suffered from the divisive
wars of the Reformation period. The royal personages take
their place against the backdrop of religious intrigue:
Mary, "the calamitous Sixth James", Charles first and
second: only the People's Army is in any way heroic
"gathering around it the peasants—especially the western
peasants—in its defence", but the defeat at Rullion Green
kills its hopes. Eventually, though, the reformation
triumphed, and the Church of Scotland came into its own.
"So doing, following an infallible law of history, it shed the
enthusiasm and high loyalty of all generous souls" (ScS
34). After this the story moves quickly: religion and politics
hopelessly mixed, Scotland intrigues and loses its way
through the second Union and the Jacobite calamities,
taking the story to Culloden. Before Hugh MacDiarmid's
"The Modern Scene", Gibbon permitted himself a final

conspectus of Scotland at 1746, and after. Prince Charlie was the end of an era:

> His final defeat at Culloden inaugurated the ruthless extirpation of the clan system in the Highlands, the extirpation of almost a whole people. Sheep-farming came to the Highlands, depopulating its glens, just as the Industrial Revolution was coming to the Lowlands, enriching the new plutocracy and brutal-izing the ancient plebs. Glasgow and Greenock were coming into being as the last embers of the old Scots culture flickered and fuffed and went out. (ScS 36)

Since then, gross darkness, "a hundred and fifty years of unloveliness and pridelessness, of growing wealth and growing impoverishment, of Scotland sharing in the rise and final torturing maladjustments of that economic system which holds all the modern world in thrall".

Much of this is deliberate overstatement: much of it plainly overlooks the analyses of authors such as Scott and Galt who must have been known to a literate and concerned Scotsman in the 1930s: some of Gibbon's views on Scotland are still controversial fifty years later. What is important in "The Antique Scene" is not whether it is correct Scottish history, but whether it gives an insight into its author's view of his Scottish heritage.

In Scottishness, as in much else, Gibbon is an enigma to the critic. Scottish history, Scottish literature and culture in its popular forms, he abhorred from the distance of Welwyn Garden City, much as he enjoyed the companion-ship of some Scottish writers such as Helen Cruickshank, Hugh MacDiarmid, and Neil Gunn. The "odd chirping and cackling of the bastardized Scots romantic schools in music and literature" (ScS 36) were the majority literary voice, while the minority which grew only slowly in public estimation were exemplified by the poetical successes of MacDiarmid—by now with the achievement of the Scottish lyrics and *A Drunk Man* behind him—and of

Helen Cruickshank, Violet Jacob, Edwin Muir. Gibbon's work also hit the minority taste, and grew in authority as it imposed a new taste by its intrinsic quality: but the resistance to be met was the traditional view of Scotland which "The Antique Scene" set out to attack scathingly. The kailyard, or merely the gently regretful, was too easy a mood for contemplating a past which seemed hopelessly receding, particularly after the cataclysmic changes of the First World War. The minister's sermon at the end of *Sunset Song* signals the end of an era as clearly as does the title of the novel—but the mood of nostalgia is hardly enough to compass Gibbon's anger at the betrayal and hurt of Scotland's history. He remembers not the fading beauty, but the cruelty and the suffering and above all the struggle. For that, chirpings and cacklings are not enough.

Gibbon's Scotland, then, was a world where the antique scene was merely a setting for a struggle in the here and now. That struggle takes several shapes, and seemingly inevitably has its internal contradictions. But one thing it firmly eschews: the return to Scottishness through political nationalism.

> ... There is an appalling number of disgusting little stretches of the globe claimed, occupied and infected by groupings of babbling little morons—babbling militant on the subjects (unendingly) of their *exclusive* cultures, their *exclusive* languages, their *national* souls, their *national* genius, their unique achievements in throat-cutting in this and that abominable little squabble in the past. ... Of all the accursed progeny of World War, surely the worst was this dwarf mongrel-litter ...
>
> ... Glasgow's salvation, Scotland's salvation, the world's salvation lies in neither nationalism nor internationalism, those twin halves of an idiot whole. It lies in ultimate cosmopolitanism, the earth the City of God, the Brahmaputra and Easter Island as

free and familiar to the man from Govan as the
Molendinar and Bute. A time will come when the
self-wrought, prideful differentiations of Scotsman,
Englishman, Frenchman, Spaniard will seem as
ludicrous as the infantile squabblings of the Heptar-
chians. A time will come when nationalism, with
other cultural aberrations, will have passed from the
human spirit, when Man, again free and unchained,
has all the earth for his footstool ... (ScS 144–6)

A very suitable co-author for Hugh MacDiarmid, Gibbon
finds himself torn between the desire to maintain a
distinctive Scottishness in life and literature, and an
inability to subscribe to the political manifestation of
Scottish nationalism. MacDiarmid, it is well known, was a
founder member of a Scottish Nationalist Party which
later ejected him for his Communism. Gibbon was
politically a Communist to the exclusion of overt nationalism, yet he plainly regretted the passing of a distinctive
Scottish culture, and explained history in terms of a
continuing struggle.

What matters in the case of Scotland, as it mattered in
the case of the land, and in the case of a continuing
civilisation, is the quality of life possible at the end of the
process. Glasgow in the Depression years is unthinkable,
and nationalist politicians, or back-to-the-Gael writers,
seemed an irrelevance to the angry author whose concern
was with the starving or the emotionally harrassed. "I'd
rather, any day, be an expatriate writing novels in Persian
about the Cape of Good Hope than a member of a
homogeneous literary cultus ..." (ScS 146–7)

The contradiction is that Gibbon, like Stevenson, could
not wholly achieve this act of voluntary exile for the sake
of his art. Physically he could remove himself, and like
Stevenson write in memory from a good geographical
distance, and probably make artistic gains as a result. Yet
the world of his imagination was haunted by specifically

Scottish symbols: land, seasons, cycles—the sound of peewits, an obvious signal in his writing about Scotland—and language. It is to language we turn for the full exploration of the contradictions in Gibbon's Scottishness.

"Literary Lights", a polemic against the state of Scottish culture in the 1930s, is one of the most entertaining pieces of journalism in *Scottish Scene*. An author who can talk of Scottish publishing houses as "generally staffed by those who in Bengali circles would write after their names, and as their chief qualification, 'failed B.A.' (or slightly worse, 'M.A. (St. Andrews)')" (ScS 196) pulls few punches, but in setting up and destroying his paper tigers, he gives his credo on the use of language.

First difficulties facing a Scottish author are those of finding a publisher in a market dominated by English firms publishing for a largely English-speaking audience. But second, there come the difficulties of the Scottish author writing in English—or what passes for English.

> The prose—or verse—is impeccably correct, the vocabulary is rich and adequate, the English is severe, serene . . . But unfortunately it is not English. The English reader is haunted by a sense of something foreign stumbling and hesitating behind this smooth façade of adequate technique: it is as though the writer did not *write* himself, but *translated* himself. (ScS 196)

That stumbling hesitancy is the desire to use a word richer, more suitable than the English equivalent: it is the desire to return to the childhood Scots, and find a word quite suitable to the occasion.

> . . . It is still in most Scots communities . . . the speech of bed and board and street and plough, the speech of emotional ecstacy and emotional stress. But it is not genteel . . . It is a thing rigorously elided from their serious intercourse—not only with the English, but

among themselves. It is seriously believed by such stratum of Scots populace to be an inadequate and pitiful and blunted implement, so that Mr. Eric Linklater delivers *ex cathedra* judgement upon it as 'inadequate to deal with the finer shades of emotion'. (ScS 196–7)

Here lies the dilemma of the Scot writing in the 1930s, as Edwin Muir was to find out very shortly with the publication of *Scott and Scotland*, a critical work which suggested that serious writing in Scotland should be in English, if it was to reach the wider audience it deserved. An argument in common currency in Scotland since the literati of Edinburgh had made similar concessions, it was a point of view quite out of keeping with the fiercer nationalist urges of Hugh MacDiarmid, whose vitriolic attack on Muir (which became a long-lasting feud) showed the strength of feeling behind the revival of a synthetic literary Scots in the nineteen-thirties.

Lewis Grassic Gibbon is here writing on the edges of a large and important controversy. On the one hand, he sees the past of his country as a long-continued dilution and diminution of distinctive and worthy characteristics, and the importance of struggle by the surviving Scots to define a Scottishness worthy of the new era. On the other hand, Gibbon firmly rejects the nationalism of his day and views Synthetic Scots with only cautious approval. "Mr MacDiarmid, like all great poets, has his in and out moments—some of them disastrous moments" (ScS 204). The liberty of a friend allows him to point out, obliquely, the extreme unevenness of much of MacDiarmid's synthetic Scots poetry. Not that Gibbon denies a very considerable achievement, but it is not the triumphant assertion of Scots as a reborn literary language.

Working in that medium of Braid Scots which he calls synthetic Scots, he has brought Scots language into

print again as a herald in tabard, not the cap-and-
bells clown of romantic versification (ScS 204).

The emphasis is again social, not political: the same
gentility which elides Scots from home conversation for a
substantial proportion of the Scottish population, relegates
it in poetry to light relief, historical atmosphere, or the
downright entertainment which music hall, as well as
kailyard, liberally produced.

Gibbon accepts the possibility that Synthetic Scots may
have a future, but hedges this future about with quali-
fications.

> When, if ever, the majority of Scots poets—not
> versifiers—begin to use Braid Scots as a medium
> that dream of a Scots literary renaissance may treat
> the *via terrena* of fulfilment, enriching (in company
> with orthodox English) the literary heritage of that
> language of Cosmopolis towards which the whole
> creation moves. (ScS 205)

First he sees the need for many talents of the nature of
MacDiarmid's, and their wholehearted acceptance of the
need for a Synthetic Scots. It is a sufficiently lukewarm
acceptance of his friend's literary Scottishness to indicate
that Gibbon's own will be different.

Novelists in the chapter are surveyed to be estimated as
at best compromise novelists between the literary wish to
be Scots, and the cultural reality of their roots. Cronin,
Gunn (who is liberally praised), Blake, Brown are
mentioned but shown to be writing from a mixed tradition, writing in English, or from "Scotshire", lacking
MacDiarmid's raging fire and desire to speak for a nation.
Gibbon's own cautiousness in relation to his national
identity is reflected in his own analysis of his work.

> [His technique] . . . is to mould the English language
> into the rhythms and cadences of Scots spoken speech,
> and to inject into the English vocabulary such

minimum number of words from Braid Scots as that remodelling requires.

So far, Gibbon notes (*Grey Granite* had not been published when the essay was written), the technique was adequate for countryside and small town: in the cities it was always possible it might degenerate, "in the fashion of Joyce, into the unfortunate unintelligibilities of a literary second childhood". (ScS 205)

The success of Gibbon's style in *A Scots Quair* is one of its most significant achievements, but in the context of the present discussion there is a different success to be signalised. By making the style mixed, the author has made the response mixed. English readers can comprehend the majority of the language, since intrusion is minimal: the language *looks* English, despite mannered rhythms and word orders, and spelling is cleverly contrived (we shall see) to disguise alien vocabulary items.

The Scottish reader, on the other hand, can recognise vocabulary items which make the story recognisably attractive, and attempted reading silently or aloud will betray familiar sentence-patterns, or ambiguous words such as "brave" and "childe" which mean one thing to a Scot, another to an English reader coming new to the prose.

The mixed response thus has a double function in conveying the author's picture of his Scotland. One important feature is that it conveys a different impression to different readers: the Scots are communicated to with an immediacy simply not possible through prose in standard English. The other feature is that the decision making on attitude, response, emotional temperature is left to the reader, who has frequently the material for a complex or highlighted response, embedded in a passage which is perfectly capable of being read at a simple level.

In this way, the author puts himself publicly in a very different position from MacDiarmid, or indeed from the

Gibbon of "Literary Lights" or "Glasgow". The ironic journalist is replaced by the ambiguous author: nationalist response, channeled through shared Scottish experience, depends on style and the individual reaction of reader to the novel. The author is not visibly seen as a participator in the process. The gain in possible audience is inestimable, for the same disgust with narrow nationalism which motivated the tirade in "Glasgow" would doubtless turn readers from openly nationalistic prose fiction.

Language, then, becomes the medium through which national feeling is channeled. Vocabulary is very sparingly used when it comes from a minority register—the same is true of *The Thirteenth Disciple* and the short stories—and the author concentrates on drawing his readers, as he does in all his fiction, into the improbable world of the story. Historical detail drew the reader to the cities of the Maya, the fields of Italy a hundred years before Christ: sharply-observed detail drew them to London, to the trenches of the War, to the Persian Dawns of the short stories set in the Middle East, to the sharply-visioned future world of *Gay Hunter*.

Gibbon wisely avoids making a separate category for Scottishness. Scottishness shares the same basic literary equipment as science fiction, history and the Far East; Scottishness is evoked through the vivid response of reader to skilful description. And *the reader* thus evokes Scottishness either from an internal reservoir of memory, or from an imagined experience skilfully constructed by the author from apparently random elements. It is not a hectic or hectoring Scottishness insisted on as a superior way of life, or a necessary qualification for the enjoyment of literature: it is the world of the book, immediate and often very hard to resist, even to those who are experiencing it at second-hand, through the author's style.

To resume: we are now in a position to approach *A Scots Quair*, with three major preparatory discussions behind us, and behind that a framework of biographical information to explain some of the contradictions implicit in Gibbon's world view.

Biographically, we have seen that he was fated to a love-hate relationship to a sharply-remembered childhood Mearns. Barred by character and inclination from full entry into its community, he was later barred by cultural distancing from the re-acceptance which plainly would have been pleasant to him. Happily settled at a distance, he yearned for the remembered pleasures of Scotland only to find them cruelly betrayed by the reality when he returned. His life thus prepares us for a view of Scotland tinged with real nostalgia, and a view of nostalgia itself tinged with scepticism, with often-betrayed expectation. The paradox of twin response to native area gives his description of rural Scotland a restless quality which goes far to hold the reader's attention or even to capture it for the first time, indicating to the non-Scot the strength of the emotion evoked by apparently barren hills.

This preliminary work is followed by an investigation into three main areas of interest in our author.

First, the land itself (in its local manifestation of Arbuthnott, but beyond that with universal implications) is seen in terms of a near-living entity, the make-believe memories of childhood transformed in manhood to a deeper sensitivity to the complexity of human response to the land as it is farmed, as it becomes the master and the farmer the slave. Beauty is evoked through sharp visual memory, through sensory impressions personal enough to be correlatives for Gibbon's memory, universal enough to function for a mixed audience—song of birds, cycle of seasons. Ugliness is evoked through human ugliness responding to the wearing-down of the pressures of the land, pressures reinforced by a social structure which exploits the small farmer to the point of exhaustion. All this complex response is evoked from the immediacy of memory, and it gives a depth to what might from a calmer perspective seem mere evocation of childhood experience.

Second, we have seen how Gibbon's mature studies took him to social history and anthropology, and through the diffusionists to a view of society and civilisation as ultimately barbaric, exploitative, degenerating forces whose removal is the ultimate hope for a world fast sinking into depression and human despair. In Scottish and non-Scottish fiction, he explores again and again the possibility of escape from "civilisation", the sensations of those who wish to escape, those who see no need.

Third, we have seen in his attitude to his own country a complex amalgam of love and hate, wholly appropriate to the author we have come to know, writing from a distance of things he feels about so acutely that he has to create a new style to transmit not only appearance, but feeling. It is in feeling about his subject that we join the strength of his emotion—and that we see the complexity of that emotion. If we feel strongly enough to accept that black and white can co-exist, then we come close to accepting the premise of Gibbon's Scottishness. His view of his times, and his native country, was too anguished by real regret to accept simplification or second-hand political commitment. He felt through the issues to the suffering people who *are* history to him: the abstract ideas are relatively meaningless, the excrescence of civilisation. But even for them he has a wary eye: at the end of "Religion" in *Scottish Scene* he points out, in 1934, that "another abortion of inactive brains—that of Fascism—looms over a tormented world," (ScS 325) and that political parties, including Scottish nationalist parties, have a danger of going that way, to enslavement with political ideas as much as with religious dogma. The danger is real, and so is the strength of emotion which writes about it, with urgency, with incoherence, with complex response. Writing at speed, often journalistically (happily so in *Scottish Scene*), mixing his modes as he satisfied the needs of a variety of editors and publishers, Gibbon strove to articulate his contending ideas clearly—clearly, without pinning them down to lifelessness. The answer came for his fiction in general, as it had come for his Scottishness in particular: it came with the creation of a literary genre sufficiently flexible, and sufficiently ambiguous, to offer the reader not a ready-made response, but the materials from which to construct a response—if possible. And the genre is wide enough to make that possibility almost universal. From this point of view, we approach *Sunset Song*, and through it the whole *Scots Quair*.

CHAPTER V

A SCOTS QUAIR

Paradoxically, it is a divided character who brings together the trilogy of *A Scots Quair*. Chris Guthrie grows to womanhood in *Sunset Song* and becomes Chris Tavendale; in *Cloud Howe* she remarries to become Chris Colquohoun; in *Grey Granite* she becomes Chris Ogilvie. The first marriage produces a son Ewan who follows his mother through the remainder of the trilogy: the second marriage produces one very short-lived child: the third is childless. In the first novel Chris marries a farmer to symbolise Scotland's link with the land; in the second a minister to symbolise the Church; in the third an unemployed countryman, drifting into the Aberdeen of the Depression years looking for a job. In *Sunset Song* there is a determined attempt to show the cataclysmic effect of the War on rural Scotland in the years 1911–1919, in *Cloud Howe* to follow the Scottish economy in the postwar early depression, in *Grey Granite* to carry the story almost into the here and now of the novel's publication in 1934. Ewan junior is grown to young manhood in *Grey Granite*, indicating that the novel can hardly be in the past at all; the dreadful scenes of poverty, unemployment and social unrest are indicative too of an unpleasant contemporaneousness.

With this weight of symbolism and representative historical and analytical intention, the trilogy might seem doomed at the least to a ponderous symmetry, at the worst to statuesque immobility. Yet nothing could be further from the truth. The author avoids the trap of making the novels *represent*. Rather he makes things happen to a heroine who herself barely knows what is going on, and

learns not to care too much. In experiencing the events of
A Scots Quair Chris learns resilience, learns a fierce independence, and learns to survive. The end, as we shall
discuss, raises almost more questions than it solves. *A Scots
Quair* is the rich-packed events of a short half-lifetime, and
it is inevitable that Chris should be dazed. The reader is in
part dazed, in part manipulated, in part educated, in part
gratified. And these conflicting emotions and ends to the
book are made possible by the splendid innovation of the
divided Chris.

> So that was the Chris and her reading and schooling,
> two Chrisses there were that fought for her heart and
> tormented her. You hated the land and the coarse
> speak of the folk and learning was brave and fine one
> day and the next you'd waken with the peewits crying
> across the hills, deep and deep, crying in the heart of
> you and the smell of the earth in your face, almost
> you'd cry for that, the beauty of it and the sweetness of
> the Scottish land and skies. (S 37)

The earlier Chris, the "Scottish" Chris, is the Chris of the
sensory impression of the land, the sharp emotive memory,
the irrational love of tradition, family, inherited language,
inherited loyalty. Her memories are of family closeness,
"tired and kind, faces dear and close to you", and her
memories too are of words, "Scots words to tell to your
heart, how they wrung it and held it, the toil of their days
and unendingly their fight". The other Chris, the
"English" one, is the girl who wants social advancement
along the terribly limited lines open to one in her age and
class: education, schoolteaching, a restrained independence within narrow socially acceptable lines. Hating the
land and the coarse speak, she expressed her aspirations by language change:

> ... you were English, back to the English words so
> sharp and clean and true—for a while, for a while, till

> they slid so smooth from your throat you knew they
> could never say anything that was worth the saying at
> all.

Already a stylistic feature is present in the preliminary
discussion which will be obvious. The author is manipulat-
ing the reader into the mind of both "Chris" characters, by
the use of "you": the reader is invited to share the emotive
response to Scotland, along with the clean-handed distaste
for peasant life inherent in the "English" characterisations.
Thus the response is not to a divided character growing up
through an adolescent identity crisis. This would be a
relatively commonplace characterisation. Rather, the
response is invited from the reader—a response from
Scottish readers against English cultural invasion, for
Scottish inherent loyalties—a response from non-Scottish
readers inviting imaginative identification with the
primary cultural feelings of the Scot for his or her own
culture, an invitation to see the "English" norm from the
opposite side, from the Scottish viewpoint to which the
English is something alien, linked to cultural values rather
than to a historical context.

Thus the divided Chris is seen very early in the book,
and above all in terms of educational attainment, and
social advancement possibilities. Chris is invited in the
school to feel pride in her advancement to the Latin class,

> above all the rest of the queans who weren't learning
> Latin or anything else, they were kitchen-maids to the
> bone.

The clever Dominie sends Chris after the visiting Inspector
(who embodies the desired cultural norms) with a
forgotten briefcase, hoping the inspector will notice his
protégée:

> . . . He gowked at her and said *Haw?* and then gave a
> bit laugh and said *Haw?* again and then *Thenks*. And
> Chris went back to the Dominie's room, the Dominie

was waiting for her and he asked if the Inspector had
given her anything, and Chris said *No*, and the
Dominie looked sore disappointed. (S 37)

There are obvious exaggerations here, but interestingly
enough the narrative tone is in colloquial Scots, indicating
a them-and-us situation in this school. The Dominie is
conspiring with Chris to draw her out of a cultural
background and implant her in another, for the sake of her
own betterment: the Inspector fails to respond, and the
Dominie's disappointment is for Chris, whose social
progress is hindered. That the story is told in the tone of
Chris and her circle emphasises the unnatural scene being
played out in the schoolroom—and by implication
throughout Scotland, creating a generation of divided
scholars seeking betterment through the same cultural tug-
of-war their novelist creator felt. The author who could
write of the language of Scots as still the tongue of bed and
board, and street and plough, was well aware of the
position of a clever girl like Chris in *Sunset Song*, and used
the polarisation of values inflicted on the children by their
educational system to contain near-irreconcilable views of
Scottish childhood in the same character. Chris lives in a
croft and endures poor living standards, family bitterness,
loss of her mother and ridicule from richer scholars, while
the feeble forces of good are represented by the Dominie,
and his praise for her essays:

the Dominie said it was fine and that sometimes she
should try to write poetry: like Mrs. Hemans. (S 38)

An educational system which can offer no more incisive
cultural assistance than this leaves Chris to find her own
cultural identity, and this suits the purpose of the trilogy
admirably. Lewis Grassic Gibbon is able to make Chris the
product of her environment, but also a self-directed
character of fixed limits which are largely self-imposed
through a series of crises experienced in her life.

Naturally the crises are approached differently as she matures, and as she gains the advantage of extraordinary self-possession, a characteristic which follows her throughout, giving her to the eyes of the world a sulky-self-possessed character which the reader knows to be little more than protective calm. Looking behind the façade, the reader is shown the emotional turmoil even in her early adolescence:

> So that was the college place at Duncairn, two Chrisses went there each morning, and one was right douce and studious and the other sat back and laughed a canny laugh at the antics of the teachers and minded Blawearie Brae and the champ of horses and the smell of dung and her father's brown, grained hands till she was sick to be home again. (S 45)

Again, the Scottish character is seen in terms of instinctive response, the English in terms of socially acquired façade. But the dour peasant self-possession remarked on by generations of hostile commentators (Gibbon must have known T. W. H. Crosland's *The Unspeakable Scot* of 1902) is easily penetrated by the author's desire to show the complex response to situation evolving in the adolescent Chris.

As she matures, so her aspirations take shape:

> Glad she'd be when she'd finished her exams and was into Aberdeen University, getting her B.A. and then a school of her own, the English Chris, father and his glowering and girning forgotten, she'd have a brave house of her own and wear what she liked and have never a man vexed with sight of her, she'd take care of that. (S 57)

The English Chris sees life in terms of clean, material things, life-denying: the Scottish Chris, on the other hand, sees the future in terms of life and the instinctive pleasures of the land; her father dead, she has £300 to buy respectability, "come out a teacher and finish with the filthy soss of the farm" (S 96), but firmly rejects the option in an emotional confrontation with her true desires.

> She walked weeping then, stricken and frightened because of that knowledge that had come on her, she could never leave it, this life of toiling days and the needs of beasts and the smoke of wood fires and the air that stung your throat so acrid, Autumn and Spring, she was bound and held as though they had prisoned her here. And her fine bit plannings!—they'd been just the dreamings of a child over toys it lacked, toys that would never content it when it heard the smore of a storm or the cry of sheep on the moors or smelt the pringling smell of a new-ploughed park under the drive of a coulter. She could no more teach a school than fly, night and day she'd want to be back, for all the fine clothes and gear she might get and hold, the books and the light and learning. (S 97–8)

The reality of the farm becomes the greater reality: although marriage and farming with Ewan feel more like a dream than reality (S 131), at least in the early years of their marriage, the crucial scene of decision just quoted is the turning point for the narrative structure of the book. Up to this point the experiencing character, the narrative filter is torn between an imposed identity and a spontaneous one. From this point onwards she will identify only with the latter, and develop from that.

The metaphors of *Sunset Song* reinforce this truth: like Lawrence and Hardy, Gibbon structured the development of his characters by reference to the seasons and the cycles of growth on the land, whether in identifying the parts of Chris's life with farming seasons ("The Unfurrowed Field", "Ploughing", "Drilling", "Seed-time", "Harvest", finally a return to "The Unfurrowed Field"), or whether identifying her own cultural identity-crisis with agricultural problems:

> Father said that the salt of the earth were the folk that drove a straight drill and never looked back, but she was no more than ploughed land still, the furrows went criss and cross, you wanted this and you wanted that, books and the fineness of them no more than an empty gabble sometimes, and then the sharn and the snapping that sickened you and drove you back to books ... (S 57)

Gibbon makes the mature Chris capable of a subconscious appreciation of the land and its problems: "You could keep at peace with the land if you gave it your heart and hands, tended it and slaved for it" (S 174). Through the complexities of the plot, suicide of mother, stroke and eventual death of father, meeting with Ewan, marriage, birth of young Ewan, War, death of husband, it is the land which is the stabilising influence on Chris. Already we see the main themes of our discussion of Gibbon at work on any attempt to approach *A Scots Quair*: land, civilisation, language and cultural values all encroach on "plot". And through it comes the idea of a divided character who struggles with conflicting emotions, and finds some sort of resolution for each struggle.

The control shown by the narrator in *Sunset Song* is nowhere more evident than in his absence, for Chris in her two conflicting personalities is usually left severely alone to make her own cultural points. At times, to be sure, there is an implied third personality, but even that is not the narrator interpolating his own point of view, but rather seen as a third, moderating Chris "that third and last Chris [who] would find voice at last for the whimsies that filled her eyes" (S 64). In the event, it is not voice that she finds, but poise: after marriage, Chris finds a new balance of personality which successfully avoids the clashes which had threatened her citadel of self earlier in the novel.

And she heard Ewan call *Ay, man, Rob*, and Rob call *Ay, man, Ewan*, and they called the truth . . . And Chris looked at them over-long, they glimmered to her eyes as though they had ceased to be there, mirages of men dreamt by a land grown desolate against its changing sky. And the Chris that had ruled those other two selves of herself, content, unquestioning these many months now, shook her head and called herself daft. (S 153)

The achievement of that third self had cost some sacrifice, some abasement to the survival standards articulated by her father when he snatched her book of stories, "*Dirt! You've more need to be down in the house helping your mother wash out the hippens*" (S 43). But not all the English Chris is lost. When Chris and her husband go to Edzell Castle, Ewan is bored, "and Chris laughed and looked at him, queer and sorry, and glimpsed the remoteness that her books had made" (S 135). That remoteness survives to become the defensive shell of character: it carries also in it memories of family dissension survived, of the hard work of the farm which Chris, like Tess of the d'Urbervilles, has to survive,

> . . . you felt like moaning like that yourself long ere the day was out and your back near cracked and broke with the strain of bending . . . (S 62)

It survives the first intimacies of marriage: when she feels the need to come to terms with her changed way of life, she must do so in isolation from her husband, sitting under the trees unseen,

> And Chris Guthrie crept out from the place below the beech trees where Chris Tavendale lay and went wandering off into the waiting quiet of the afternoon, Chris Tavendale heard her go, and she came back to Blawearie never again (S 137).

The preserved core of privacy helps the reader, it helps Chris survive repeated assaults credibly, it helps prepare the reader psychologically for the breakdown of Chris's

marriage and the subsequent reintegration of her
personality—and three times over this is necessary, in the
course of the trilogy.

Curious, avant-garde, little liked, an outsider from her
community, intense, loyal, withdrawn, Chris is a thing of
contradictions and as such an excellent vehicle for a novel
which seeks to convey cultural complexities as well as
merely a picture of Scottish country life in wartime. What
of our first main field of interest in Gibbon's work, the
Land in *Sunset Song*?

Unforgettably, the Land in *Sunset Song* is characterised
as Kinraddie, the childhood village for Chris, as for her
creator—despite claims to the contrary a clear and
unflattering picture of Arbuthnott remembered from a
distance which gives clarity and artistic shape to the
immediacy of childhood experience. The narrative voice
which introduces Kinraddie to the reader has the mixture
of styles we already recognise from Gibbon, the conversa-
tional tone of the peasant *raconteur*, with the appeal directly
from the writer to the reader on a level the implied peasant
perhaps would not see or understand.

> So that was Kinraddie that bleak winter of nineteen
> eleven and the new minister, him they chose early
> next year, he was to say it was the Scots countryside
> itself, fathered between a kailyard and a bonny brier
> bush in the lee of a house with green shutters. And
> what he meant by that you could guess at yourself if
> you'd a mind for puzzles and dirt, there wasn't a
> house with green shutters in the whole of Kinraddie.
> (S 31)

The peasant was not to know of Ian Maclaren and *Beside
the Bonnie Brier Bush*, the Kailyard best-seller, any more
than he would know of George Douglas Brown's *The House
with the Green Shutters*. But the reader would, and the writer
communicates a view of Kinraddie, through the supposed
characterisation of the minister, around the narrator,

straight to the reader. The minister's meaning, no doubt, included the reference to Kinraddie as *looking* like kail-yard, in its pastoral simplicity, and also to Kinraddie actually *being* a hotbed of scandal and gossip, such as the Barbie which George Douglas Brown filled with his ver-sions of the "Scot malignant".

Certainly the minister has an apt description of his own parish as a setting for such a novel as *Sunset Song*. The strength of the kailyard village as a setting was its timelessness; lacking the challenge of change (a challenge present in Galt's Dalmailing) the kailyard village could allow human characterisation full scope without too much distraction—and this was the chief pleasure of the kailyard, along with the reliving of pleasant Scottish historical scenes and picturesque customs. Undeniably such features exist in Kinraddie, and make it (like Barbie) superficially a kailyard village, slightly remote and cut off from the railway, dominated by a few powerful person-alities, strongly patriarchal, clinging to Churchgoing and the public forms of Christianity, farming in the old way and liking it.

Where both Barbie and Kinraddie differ is that the novelist is out to puncture the initial timelessness of the impression—to undercut the kailyard assumptions too common in their culture, by showing that Scotland is about here and now, about change and response to change, rather than endless repetitions of a commercially successful formula like the kailyard idylls. There is material very early in *Sunset Song* to suggest the process of change and redistribution which is to be accelerated by war, and intensified into *Cloud Howe*; the powerful families of the area are losing their grip, and more important, even before the great war, the improving landowners are changing the ways of traditional farming.

> ... He had bigger steadings built and he let them at bigger rents and longer leases, he said the day of the

fine big farm had come. And he had woods of fir and
larch and pine planted to shield the long, bleak slopes,
... (S 17)

By the end of *Sunset Song*, the pace of change is accelerating,
and by *Cloud Howe*, when Chris revisits Blawearie with her
second husband,

> ... She could smell the winter smell of the land and
> the sheep they pastured now on Blawearie, in the
> parks that once came rich with corn that Ewan had
> sown and they both had reaped, where the horses had
> pastured, their kye and their stock ... (S 207)

By *Grey Granite*, the process is merely implied, an
irrelevance beside the greater concerns of the city.

A tension thus exists, and must be acknowledged at
the outset, between the pastoral externals of Kinraddie,
recognised as part-kailyard by the cynical minister, and
the hidden but undeniable forces of change which grow
in Kinraddie even as Chris grows. The Guthries are
incomers, and they bring new ways, in the sense that John
Guthrie brings machines to help the work—and keep
down labour costs, pointing the way forward even though
the actual machine he uses is old and cheap (S 61). The
scene is most reminiscent of *The Mayor of Casterbridge*, and
the battle of wills between Farfrae (who welcomes the
machines) and Henchard (who ridicules them): the future
lies with the machine, but the attraction of the centuries-
old way is undeniable and given full prominence. It is
interesting in this to compare Brown with Gibbon: in *The
House with The Green Shutters* the old ways are swept aside by
change, but the old ways are as uniformly ridiculed as the
new. In *Sunset Song*, in the opening scenes, Kinraddie is
changing reluctantly in keeping with human nature and
the desire for continuity, and change will be forced only by
economic necessity, and the greater threat posed by the
War.

John Guthrie, Chris's father, is an important indicator of Kinraddie attitudes. He has something of the fierce dedication of the farmer in *Clay* who allowed his wife to die while he tended his land obsessively,

> weeds yammered out of Blawearie soil like bairns from a school at closing time, it was coarse, coarse land, wet, raw, and red clay, father's temper grew worse the more he saw of it. (S 54)

An intelligent man, he hints at a breadth of vision, given a less punishing work schedule, and a more relaxed attitude to time and society.

> For the bitterness had grown and eaten away into the heart of him in his year at Blawearie. So coarse the land proved in the turn of the seasons he'd fair been staggered . . . Now also it grew plain to him here as never in Echt that the day of the crofter was fell near finished, put by, the day of folk like himself . . . the last of the farming folk that wrung their living from the land with their own bare hands . . .

Significantly, it is "the land he loved better than his soul or God", and there is clear implication that he loved it much better than he loved his family, to whom his affection is stinted. (S 67)

Here in John Guthrie, even before we consider the deeper implications of his character, is a modifier of any early implication that Kinraddie is a pastoral idyll. Kinraddie is one of the features which twist Guthrie to the merciless tyrant who looms over Chris's school years: Kinraddie denies him ease and relaxation, and gives him only the companionship of Chae and Long Rob, while most of the men of Kinraddie are of purely secondary interest. Significantly, Guthrie is dead by the end of the novel, and the war picks off the men who were capable of engaging his intellectual attention—Chae and Rob—along with the younger men capable of taking on the

heartbreak and challenge of farming in the old style—
James Leslie, Ewan Tavendale. A clear attempt by the
author to puncture the kailyard idyll seems undeniable.
The Kinraddie way of life is in sunset as the novel opens,
and the sunset deepens throughout. It is not just War but a
way of life, which moves unperceived but tragically off-
stage.

Permanence is something difficult to come by in *Sunset
Song*, not just in the rapid evolutions of the plot (the
disposal of the Guthrie family by death, suicide and
resettlement is abrupt in the extreme) but in the
philosophical positions adopted by Chris.

> And then a queer thought came to her there in the
> drooked fields, that nothing endured at all, nothing
> but the land she passed across, tossed and turned and
> perpetually changed below the hands of the crofter
> folk since the oldest of them had set the Standing
> Stones by the loch of Blawearie ... Sea and sky and
> the folk who wrote and fought and were learnéd,
> teaching and saying and praying, they lasted but as a
> breath, a mist of fog in the hills, but the land was
> forever, it moved and changed below you, but was
> forever, you were close to it and it to you, not at a
> bleak remove it held you and hurted you. And she had
> thought to leave it all! (S 97)

The thought pursues Chris throughout the trilogy after
that moment, even on the eve of her wedding to Ewan:

> This marriage of hers was nothing, that it would pass
> on and forward into days that had long forgotten it ...
> (S 116)

It finds horrifying confirmation in the thunder scene where
the horse is killed by lightning, to be discovered by Chris
who alone in the house has the courage to face The Land in
this mood:

> Then she saw that the barbed wire was alive, the
> lightning ran and glowed along it, a living thing, a
> tremulous, vibrant serpent that spat and glowed and
> hid its head and quivered again to sight. If the horses
> stood anywhere near to that they were finished . . .
> (S 105)

If the Land, as actor, can have a positive role, it can also
suffer, as Kinraddie does in a physical sense early in the
war, with the cutting of the trees. Kinraddie folk see the
benefit of the woodsmen, the high board prices they pay,
the profit of the trees; Chae the farmer sees the price he will
pay with the shelter of the woods lost, the fields laid open to
the winds. Again, as in the kailyard example, Gibbon
cleverly presents the conflicting attitudes through the
mind of a peasant narrator not quite capable of appreciat-
ing the complexity.

> Chae shouted *What, others?* and went out to look; and
> when he came back he didn't shout at all, he said he'd
> often minded of them out there in France, the woods,
> so bonny they were, and thick and grave, fine shelter
> and lithe for the cattle. Nor more than that would he
> say, it seemed then to Kirsty that he quietened down,
> and was quiet and queer all his leave, it was daft to let
> a bit wood go vex him like that. (S 155)

The intense beauty of the memory of Kinraddie means
intolerably strong emotion to Chae in the trenches, as
obviously it did to Ewan (S 180) when he deserted: the
raping of the woods for short-term gain is the betrayal of
Kinraddie almost as a living thing, even if the narrative
voice is insensitive to its own emotive content.

But then the War, the great impersonal force of this book
(as distinct from the "only half-inanimate" rigs of the
Kinraddie land) has the power to distort centuries of
tradition, and to do it through the abruptness of saw and
axe, and the more subtle forces of changing the minds of

Kinraddie. Chris's response to the news of her husband's death in France typifies much of Kinraddie's attitude to the war, exactly caught to explain their incomprehension of the wider issues outside the novel.

> *Country and King? You're havering, havering! What have they to do with my Ewan, what was the King to him, what their damned country? Blawearie's his land, it's not his wight that others fight wars!* (S 178)

This is the end of a process which Gibbon skilfully weaves into *Sunset Song*, a process beginning with Chae Strachan's excited announcement to Chris and Ewan that the newspapers were talking of war, "But Chris didn't care and Ewan didn't either, so Chae took himself off with his paper again" (S 144). Ewan is totally unconcerned about the wider issues, concerned only with the speed of his crops in Blawearie: "Chris paid no heed to the war, there were aye daft devils fighting about something or other".

What Kinraddie does notice is when the war comes to its doorstep, when sugar goes up in price, when James Leslie enlists for the army, and "folk thought him fair daft, showing off and looking for a holiday, just" (S 148). Chris herself notices not then, but when her own personal friend Chae is next to enlist: but her main concerns are about hoarding sugar for jam, not about the war. The minister's sermons interest the community much more than the war to which they refer.

> But Ewan didn't care one way or the other, as he told to Chris. The minister might be right or be wrong with his Babylons and whores and might slobber Attila every night of the week, Blawearie had its crop all in and that was what mattered. And Chris said *Yes, what a blither about a war, isn't it, Ewan?* and tickled young Ewan as he lay on her lap . . . (S 149)

Corn and cattle prices are good: the war actually pleases Chris and Ewan (S 152) until the example of Chae stirs

Ewan to emulation (S 153) and he finally succumbs to
social pressure, ". . . grown sick of it all, folk laughing and
sneering at him for a coward, Mutch and Munro aye
girding at him" (S 162). Mutch and Munro, of course, do
not themselves go to the war, but stay in Kinraddie to
profit from high farming prices, to turn to intensive
farming and market gardening, to adapt to short-term
demand. They survive: those like Chae and Ewan, and
finally Rob, who make the greater gesture and risk leaving
Kinraddie, are the ones whom fate destroys.

What Gibbon does emphasise is the closed nature of the
community in Kinraddie. While its inhabitants remain
there, their views are as narrowed as the narrator's in
Chris's mind, their ideas about politics and religion frozen
in the nineteenth century, their desire for change almost
eliminated. Only exceptional spirits like Chae and Rob
are free enough to have exceptional views, Chae's for
Socialism and political involvement, Rob's for atheism
and pacificism. The community, inevitably, laughs at
them for being different. What is more pessimistic is that,
while we admire them for their stand in being different
(and for being Chris's closest friends) we also see them cut
down, of all the Kinraddie men, by the war. In this too,
Gibbon seems to be predicting the end of the Kinraddie
way of life, for in a peacetime Kinraddie it is from Chae
and Rob that the stimulus of the community comes, in the
wedding celebrations, the funeral, the arguments at table
in harvest home. Left without them, Kinraddie is reduced
to the *nouveaux riches* who have profiteered from the war, or
the ruined farmers who leave surreptitiously at the end
when the heritors decide to sell the farms to the sitting
tenants—if the tenants have the money.

Thus Kinraddie is a complex backdrop to the story of
Chris. On the surface a comfortable kailyard village, it
seethes with human conflict in a manner quite credible
without being overdone. The bitterness of *The House with
the Green Shutters* is balanced by the sympathetic characters

like Chae and Rob, by the narrative core of Chris herself, and by the intensely lyrical interludes which are felt through the sensory perceptions of the "Scottish" Chris, giving Kinraddie an attractiveness which Barbie could never have, seen as it is through the coldly cynical eye of its narrator throughout.

Part of the complexity of Kinraddie, we have seen, lies in the continuing design of the author to make the land part-animate, an actor in the tragedy. It thus takes its share in moulding the character of Chris's father, and in determining the final direction of Chris's own evolving Scottishness, by ensuring that the land-loving "Scottish" Chris makes the final decisions, and pushes the essentially alien English equivalent beneath the surface.

Yet the community itself is animate, and changes in two ways which have been demonstrated. One is a wholly natural process of change and evolution, which is in motion before the novel begins, and is accelerated by later events. Another is a cataclysmic and speeded-up set of changes induced by wartime conditions, changes which are still in progress at the end of the novel, and which form the core of the minister's address at the unveiling of the Standing Stones.

If, with the Standing Stones, we pass to our second line of enquiry, we find that Gibbon's concern with civilisation goes far to explain some of the more baffling features of *Sunset Song*.

Civilisation impinges (as did the War) in different ways for different people. For example Arbuthnott, Kinraddie, has its share of "naturals", people whose mental state is not sufficient to warrant hospitalisation, but who lived harmlessly among the normal farming community. To them, Kinraddie has become normality, and they form part of the normality of a complex society. They may know shorthand, make references to ideas that are unexpected, hint of an existence outside Kinraddie. Oddly, they are more "civilised" than many people who have lived in

Kinraddie all their lives. Their existence in the novel is typical of the oblique ways in which the author inserts outside forces into a closed world.

Another is the mere arrival of Chris and her family from Aberdeenshire, sent to Kinraddie and to a move through civilisation—the encounter between Guthrie (in his previous farm) and a new-fangled motor car (representing civilisation), an angry encounter which resulted in a forced move for the Guthries. Aberdeenshire in this novel is throughout seen in terms of innocence before the troubles of the present civilised time—the Echt land was easier to farm, Chris's mother had fewer children and found life easier, John Guthrie's character was less soured.

There is an important, and surprisingly little studied moment in the novel where the point about Kinraddie representing "civilisation" to Chris is made quite clearly to the reader who bears the wider context of Gibbon's work in mind—Gibbon the writer of science-fiction, Gibbon obsessed with time and the possibility of time travel, Gibbon the cultural historian and anthropologist.

> For out of the night ahead of them came running a man, father didn't see him or heed to him, though old Bob ... snorted and shied. And as he came he wrung his hands, he was mad and singing, a foreign creature, black-bearded, half-naked he was; and he cried in the Greek *The ships of Pytheas! The ships of Pytheas!* and went by into the smore of the sleet-storm on the Grampian Hills, Chris never saw him again . . . (S 41–2)

Chris thinks she is having a dream, but in reality she has this flash of perception while the whole family is struggling up the high hill road which will take them down to the Mearns. It is snowing, and people's minds are on other things, though significantly Chris is sensitive enough to the moment, and Bob the horse is too—one recalls the repeated legendary sensitivity of horses to devils and

supernatural occurrences not noticed by humans. Clearly
Gibbon is suggesting in this scene a native Scot, a Pict
probably, terror-stricken at the first sight of the Greek
civilisation brought by the explorer Pytheas to the shores of
Scotland, and comparing the response to that of Chris,
embarking on her own voyage of exploration in the
Mearns. The details are a little askew—the savage would
be crying in his own language, not in Greek—but the
implication is clear. Innocence is passing, grief is expressed
by the wringing of hands and violence of emotion,
civilisation is about to take over.

   Similarly, there is the encounter between Chae and a
Roman soldier in the moonlight, not long before Chae
leaves for his last tour of duty in the War, the tour that kills
him. Chae cried

> . . . *Good night, then.* But there wasn't an answer, so he
> looked again, and no cart was there, the shingly stones
> shone white and deserted under the light of the moon,
> the peewits were crying away in the distance. And
> Chae's hackles fair stood up on end, for it came on him
> that it was no cart of the countryside he had seen, it
> was a thing of light wood or basket-work, battered
> and bent, low behind, with a pole and two ponies . . .
> . . . And maybe it was one of the men of old time that
> he saw there, a Calgacus' man from the Graupius
> battle when they fought the Romans up from the
> south; or maybe it had only been the power of Long
> Rob's Glenlivet . . . (S 158)

Maybe a dream, maybe a lightheaded moment, but
both these encounters are with vanished civilisation which
is basically cruel and bodes ill to those whose later fates
it mirrors. The Roman soldier was doubtless on his way
to death at Mons Graupius (Gibbon, a keen amateur
archaeologist, would have been as likely as any to try to
locate that enigmatic battle near Stonehaven, the generally accepted theory) and Chae to death in a later quarrel

in France; the early Scot faced enslavement of body or mind (or both) to a new civilisation, as does Chris arriving in Kinraddie. The two scenes in the book are easy to overlook, but taken in the context of *Three Go Back* and *Gay Hunter*, they make unambiguous and hostile statements about the Scottish civilisation Chris can know in her lifetime.

The Standing Stones are less understudied, but perhaps also underestimated. They belong to a vanished civilisation—this much we know, and even Gibbon does not try accurately to place them, for their history was little known in his day. What is certain is that some kind of civilisation reared them, and that Gibbon grew up familiar with several examples of the form, including one near his home—a circle which has, like Blawearie Loch, unfortunately vanished in the name of progress.

The Stones are timeless, ageless: they point their shadows "maybe just as they'd done of an evening two thousand years before when the wild men climbed the brae and sang their songs in the lithe of those shadows" (S 54–5) and they bring a shiver to Chris when she sees them. But they have another, less enigmatic function: they provide a haven, a refuge from modern civilisation thanks to their very timelessness.

> She leant against it, the bruised cheek she leaned and it was strange and comforting—stranger still when you thought that this old stone circle, more and more as the years went on at Kinraddie, was the only place where ever she could come and stand back a little from the clamour of the days. (S 89)

She chooses this comfort at times of extreme stress, when her father becomes unbearable in his last illness (S 89), when Ewan and she quarrel before the pregnancy is confirmed (S 140), when she has her supreme vision of Ewan's return from death after the war (S 182)—these important moments have the common property that they are perceived either in physical contact with the Standing Stones, or in close proximity to them.

Thus civilisation and time are linked, and through that link also comes a link with the Land, for the Land is semi-animate and timeless, and so the Stones and the Land together form a backdrop to the human action which is removed from human passion, removed from the constraints of time and patience, removed from love and hate. The Stones are there at the arrival at Kinraddie, they are the last things we see in *Sunset Song*, and the land visible below them is similarly unchanging, despite the change in human patterns. The minister's closing oration is delivered from the Standing Stones, and the supreme irony of the book is that the stones should be chosen for the monument to the men killed in a war which civilisation forced on an unwilling Kinraddie.

But civilisation brought more than war to Kinraddie, it brought mental stress in a form which also involves consideration of John Guthrie. For the Diffusionist Gibbon saw religion as one of civilisation's inventions, and its continuance as one of the necessary evils of civilisation till (as the essay on religion in *Scottish Scene* makes plain) men are again free enough in their minds to enjoy a Blakean Jerusalem, a state of freedom where they can do without the restraints and the constraints of religion. Lacking a view of religion as a historical supernatural process, Gibbon sees it as a superimposed system which affects the mass of people who do not understand it, yet cling tenaciously to its outside observances and resent change in religion, while feeling very little true identification with it.

The ambiguous nature of religion could be discussed in terms of the pecadillos of the ministers Kinraddie knows in the course of *Sunset Song*, but it could more usefully be seen through John Guthrie, since we see him at close quarters through Chris, and not in the public eye where his iron control very rarely permits feelings to be seen.

At the outset of the story John and Jean Guthrie are an attractive pair in Aberdeenshire, their marriage a thing of spontaneous love, sustained by mutual attraction, the work of the land hard but bearable. It is the interference of religious, or quasi-religious, ideas with this spontaneous life which brings discord. "She was sweet and kind to him", but "his face would go black with rage at her because of that sweetness that tempted his soul to hell" (S 34). John Guthrie is thus to be understood throughout in terms of a struggle between a very strong sexual urge, and a very strong intellectualised restraint to that urge, the unnatural self-possession breaking out in various eccentricities or perversions. Even the children are aware of the arguments in bed, *Four of a family's fine: there'll be no more.* And father thundered at her, that way he had, *Fine? We'll have what God in His mercy may send us, woman. See you to that* (S 34). The sexual drive manifests itself in sadism, brutal treatment to young Will (Chris's brother), openly sexual threats for misuse of the name of Jehovah, "... *if I ever hear you again take your Maker's name in vain, if I ever hear you use that word again, I'll libb you. Mind that. Libb you like a lamb*" (S 36). Beatings, sneerings, sexual jealousy characterise his treatment of his son, and Chris herself feels threatened by his enormous, unsatisfied sexual appetite:

> *He shamed you then?* he whispered; and Chris shook her head and at that father seemed to go limp and his eyes grew dull. *Ah well, it's the kind of thing that would happen in a godless parish like this.* (S 51)

John Guthrie's sister stabs him directly: "... *It'll be long ere I have to kill myself because my man beds me like a breeding sow*; and father said *You dirty bitch*" (S 60). But there is an unnatural appetite, the appetite that sends him to his own daughter's bedroom door in the night (S 64–5), that breaks out in unreasoning anger at Will's running away (S 86), that pays for it in a paralytic stroke (S 87) though even then (S 90) Chris fears assault in the night from her own father, paralytic though he is,

> like a great frog struggling, squattering across the
> floor, thump, thump on the stairs, coming down on
> her while she slept, that madness and tenderness there
> in his eyes (S 90)

Obviously, we can blame this on overstimulated sexual
appetite, unnaturally repressed by religious training. To
blame anything too simply would be an injustice to the
book: John Guthrie is a figure writ large to make a point,
and one cannot blame his maladjustment simply on the
Church of his time (which imposed standards for the good
of society, which John Guthrie chose to interpret his own
way) nor simply his own character, for it was undoubtedly
influenced by the morality which surrounded him.

Gibbon adds to these partial explanations another
one—the forces of civilisation. Inevitably, Chris sees her
father clearly only when he is dead, and the coffin is being
interred.

> And she minded the long roads he's tramped to the
> kirk with her when she was young, how he'd smiled at
> her and called her his lass in days before the world's
> fight and the fight of his own flesh grew over-bitter,
> and poisoned his love to hate . . .

> [she could remember] all the fine things of him that
> the years had hidden from their sight, the fleetness of
> him and his justice, and the fight unwearying he'd
> fought with the land and its masters to have them all
> clad and fed and respectable, he'd never rested
> working and chaving for them, only God had beaten
> him in the end. (S 95)

Which is to say, he had died—or the Church had beaten
him. The ambiguity is left for the reader's decision.

Against this vision of a man whom civilisation has
ruined, there is the initial freshness of Chris's husband
Ewan, spokesman for the new generation of small tenant

farmers, inheritor of John Guthrie's Blawearie and his
savings. Ewan appears to have the virtues of John Guthrie,
without his vices; wedded to the land, capable of endless
physical labour for the land, instinctive in his approach to
farming, instinctive in his loyalty to wife and family, he
appears the ideal husband to a Scottish Chris who has
made her commitment to the way of life with which *Sunset
Song* began.

Simply to have such a figure killed would be far too
simple: first the author has to degrade him, and this is
achieved in the brief training period at Lanark which sends
Ewan back to Kinraddie bestialised almost beyond
recognition. There is certainly some suggestion earlier in
the book that Ewan has a powerful sexual appetite, but no
suggestion since his marriage that he retained lust in that
form—till he comes back coarsened in mind and in body, a
thing of horror to a Chris who can barely tolerate his
company, and who is frankly glad to see him go to his army
duty. His responses are those of a beast: *"Hell, Chris, what a
bloody place!"* (S 169)—from the man who had married the
farm, along with Chris, to all outward appearances a few
pages earlier. When Ewan opines *"I'd have done better to spend
the night with a tart in the town"* (S 170) he is driving a nail
between him and Chris. Chris, with her son young Ewan
and her work at Blawearie, has retained her separateness
from civilisation: provincial and small-town though her
attitude to the war is, the author invites us to contrast it
with even brief exposure to the values reigning in the big
world outside—Lanark, the army, France. The scene is
seen entirely from Chris's point of view, and the response
we feel can be only one of horror.

It is instructive to compare Ewan's bestial return to
Blawearie with that of the intelligent and sensitive Will,
home on leave and revisiting scenes of his youth.

> Chris said *But you'll come back, you and Mollie, to bide in
> Scotland again?* and Will laughed, he seemed still a

> mere lad in spite of his foreign French uniform, *Havers,*
> *who'd want to come back to this country? It's dead or it's*
> *dying—and a damned good job!* (S 165)

Will sees what is wrong, in the context of Blawearie: he
is still committed to farming, and the future lies in the
large-scale farming which he can aspire to overseas, but
hopelessly lacks the capital for in Scotland. His dismissal of
Scotland is clear-eyed and unsentimental, anticipative of
Ewan junior's dismissal of Scotland at the end of *Grey
Granite*, pleasant no doubt to remember but essentially
unimportant in the context of the social problems of the
twentieth century.

Ewan senior has no such responses because he simply
lacks the equipment to intellectualise as does Will. He
realises, too late, his mistake in leaving Blawearie, in
betraying Chris, but as he reports them to Chae out in
France, under sentence of death for desertion, his feelings
were instinctive, sensational:

> *Mind the smell of dung in the parks on an April morning,*
> *Chae? And the peewits over the rigs? Bonny they're flying this*
> *night in Kinraddie, and Chris sleeping there, and all the Howe*
> *happed in mist . . .* (S 180)

What Ewan senior lacks is his wife's ability to adapt: she
has struggled for her adaptation, but it tides her through
her contacts with this demeaning civilisation, and she
retains a citadel of identity to preserve her sanity. Ewan
acts instinctively and fails.

*   *   *

Will dismissing the idea of returning to Blawearie, Ewan
remembering the sights and sounds of a native Scotland,
Chae stricken at the cutting of the trees on his land—they
represent versions of Scottishness which lead us to the third
part of our consideration of *Sunset Song*, which is very much
about versions of Scottishness. Unveiling the war memorial at the end of the novel, the minister specifically makes

the point that the men who died were *"the Last of the Peasants, the Last of the Old Scots folk"* (S 193).

What he means by that is expanded in the beautifully written oration which concludes the novel.

> *A new generation comes up that will know them not, except as a memory in a song, they passed with the things that seemed good to them with loves and desires that grow dim and alien in the days to be. It was the old Scotland that perished then, and we may believe that never again will the old speech and the old songs, the old curses and the old benedictions, rise but with alien effort to our lips.*

> *The last of the peasants, those four that you knew, took that with them to the darkness and the quietness of the places where they sleep. And the land changes, their parks and their steadings are a desolation where the sheep are pastured, we are told that great machines come soon to till the land, and the great herds come to feed on it, the crofter has gone, the man with the house and the steading of his own and the land closer to his heart than the flesh of his body. Nothing, it has been said, is true but change, nothing abides . . .* (S 193)

The new minister is a sympathetic character, we are predisposed to accept his view: he articulates what we can see emerging as the concensus view, the view of Kinraddie from the outside but with inside knowledge—the view, in short, shared by the Minister (inside the community, yet not of it) and the reader who has been installed in Kinraddie via the narrative medium of Chris Guthrie/Tavendale. And that Scottish community is threatened by varieties of change both obvious and subtle.

The Land has taken its toll; the large farms are taking over, population redistribution is inevitable. The civilisation which brought the war has taken its toll, in trees and in men. But can the old Scotland of Kinraddie that looked so settled and so beautiful, the Kinraddie of pre-war 1911, even return? We now know that it is impossible, both because the characters who sustained it have gone, and because the patterns of agriculture would no longer sustain it in the form it then had. Small farms are uneconomic, and small farmers can no longer find labour—with its new mobility, labour expresses its freedom in terms echoed by Will Guthrie's rejection of Kinraddie as a place for a future and raising a family. Crofting, bothying are dead. And a way of life is apparently swept away.

Yet that would be too easy, and it would quite fail to account for the emotional power of the novel's ending, several generations on into the process which the minister is describing in his speech. He is not describing the end of Scotland—but the end of Old Scotland. Even in Chris's time (Gibbon's time) versions of Scotland which were essentially ersatz were commonplace, the Scotland of Pootie and his Burns recitation, the Dominie with his milk-and-water Mrs Hemans, the educational system with its uncertainties between Scotland and England.

Chris, as always, occupies central territory, not showing her hand, listening to all, accepting no-one's version wholeheartedly. Yet she has considerable insight into genuine sources of Scottish culture. Her father's Scottish Presbyterian culture is more authentic than the ill-chosen books the minister offers her from the Manse library (S 54–6). Her mother's songs, her own acquaintance with folk song, leads her to reflections on Scottish music far more authentic than the lightweight culture Aberdeen has to offer her age-group, in *Grey Granite*—like the cinema scene (S 415). Rather at her own wedding reception,

> ... it came on Chris how strange was the sadness of Scotland's singing, made for the sadness of the land and sky in dark autumn evenings, the crying of men and women of the land who had seen their lives and loves sink away in the years, things wept for beside the sheep-buchts, remembered at night and in twilight. The gladness and kindness had passed, lived and

forgotten, it was Scotland of the mist and rain and the crying sea that made the songs . . . (S 130)

The "sugary surge of *Auld Lang Syne*" on the same page is a deliberate contrast to this low-key, authentic culture to which Chris has surely instinctive access through her mother, through her upbringing and schooling. Like her creator, she knew this Scottish literature without trying, certainly with little help from her educational system.

Significantly, the cultural inheritance is a shared one, for the climatic experience of the unveiling of the war memorial is performed to the playing, on the pipes, of *The Flouers o the Forest*, the same song Chris sang at her wedding (with obvious symbolism), yet the song which affects people as widely on this different occasion as it did then. The affecting music penetrates the defences of all listeners:

> It rose and rose and wept and cried, that crying for the men who fell in battle . . . the young ploughmen they stood with glum, white faces, they'd no understanding or caring, it was something that vexed and tore at them, it belonged to times they had no knowing of. (S 194)

This is what is important about their Scottishness: even after the war, the best of the Kinraddie community taken away by the impersonal forces of an un-Scottish civilisation, the effects of the correct Scottish stimulus will still bring a response, even a totally irrational one like that evoked by the pipe tune. Scottishness is still possible, but increasingly (as the minister puts it) with "alien effort".

> *It was the old Scotland that perished then, and we may believe that never again will the old speech and the old songs, the old curses and the old benedictions, rise but with alien effort to our lips.* (S 193)

Sunset Song, as analysed so far in this chapter, could best be summed up as an attempt to short-circuit this "alien effort", to evoke a response as direct from the Scot as the pipe tune—and perhaps some response as direct even from the reader without the primary Scottish experience in the background.

The Scottish response is gained not mainly by music (which is reserved largely for festival occasions), but by speech, and here Gibbon writes in a discussion which exemplifies the problem of the Scottish ordinary person in the early twentieth century, the problem confronting Gibbon in his "Literary Lights" essay from *Scottish Scene*: Long Rob of the Mill, lamenting the demise of spoken Scots, bemoans the absence of English synonyms.

> And Rob said *You can tell me, man, what's the English for sotter, or greip, or smore, or pleiter, gloaming or glanching or well-henspeckled? And if you said gloaming was sunset you'd fair be a liar; and you're hardly that, Mr Gordon* (S 123)

Inevitably, perhaps, Gibbon fixed on the obvious word "gloaming", untranslatable—but the general point Long Rob makes here is valid and would find many Scots to agree with it even in the 1980s. Language is the tool which permits the primary, the near-simultaneous Scottish response. Lacking that tool, the writer is unmanned as is the Scottish author writing in English described in "Literary Lights"—he translates himself, rather than writing.

Sunset Song has a clear function to act as catalyst for Scottish readers, to enable (or to revive) the primacy of response to Scottish experience by describing it in such a way that either exact memory of Scottish experience is awakened in the reader, or (and this may also be available to non-Scots) that the scene is so vividly recreated that the non-Scot allows himself to feel it simultaneously in the imagination—thinks himself into Scotland, in short. This may account for the novel's success overseas, even in translation; it certainly could be argued to account for the success with which *Sunset Song*, and the short stories, translated to the medium of television.

In performing this function, *Sunset Song* achieves its excellence: the removal of the "alien effort" of Scottishness for Scots, and the reduction of it for non-Scots to the point where artistically it can be overlooked. The strategies for this are two-fold—one is the manipulation of Scottish situation, the other the manipulation of Scottish speech.

Situation is strongly biased to the international and the universal. Births and deaths, marriages, the cycles of the land, the neighbourhood experience of Kinraddie—the flavour may be Scottish and the community spirit evoked certainly so, but Gibbon is cleverly appealing to scenes which will capture the attention of an audience who has not known these emotions in a Scottish context, but certainly in their own home context. Interestingly enough, in so doing he was following George Douglas Brown's example, wittingly or otherwise, in *The House with the Green Shutters*: the kailyard scenes and situations which that novel describes, yet perverts to show the ridiculousness of the kailyard treatment, are repeated in *Sunset Song*, in setting, in major characters, in father-daughter-son relations, in homecoming, in the stress on education. The kailyard situations were universal in appeal, and Brown and Gibbon cleverly use the market for such situations for their own purposes. One could compare Neil Gunn's choice of situation in the opening of *Highland River*, or the community fishing spirit evoked in *The Silver Darlings*, to see the same response being searched for—not alien effort but spontaneous, or apparently spontaneous, Scottish response.

In language, as Long Rob and Mr Gordon argue, things are more difficult to discuss, since there is a vocabulary barrier to be crossed before intelligibility is possible. Gibbon, of course, left us in *Scottish Scene* his own brief definition of his technique:

> ... to mould the English language into the rhythms and cadences of Scots spoken speech, and to inject

into the English vocabulary such minimum number
of words from Braid Scots as that remodelling
requires. (ScS 205)

There, in essence, is the technique by which he seeks to
bypass the "alien effort", and produce something auth-
entically Scottish. In the example from Long Rob the
number of Scottish words is at a maximum, for Rob (and
Gibbon) are making a point about the survival of Scottish
vocabulary in daily speech: such words come rarely in
Gibbon's style, rarely enough not seriously to inhibit the
non-Scots reader of his prose. Some are repetitive, barely
disguised from standard English (and therefore not
offputting) though their meaning may be significantly
changed:

coarse (coorse): rough
brave (braw): fine
childe (chiel): man
silver (siller): money
quean (quine): girl

Some are more notably Scots, and perhaps obsolescent:

gey: very
orra: unpleasant, unusual, odd
peesie: peewit
cry: call

Sometimes the effect is achieved more by rhythms and
sentence structures than by vocabulary changes, as when
inversions and rearrangements make the sentence distinctively not English.

Then Maidie knew, as she watched Chris at work,
and tweetered the news to some quean outbye, and
the quean gasped *Never!* and told Ag Moultrie, the
Roarer and Greeter, met in the street. (S 302)

The only creature that seemed to flourish as the
harvest brought a dour end to the weather and the

> clouds rolled slower over the Howe was Will Melvin that kept the Segget Arms, him and that sharp-tongued besom his wife, the spinners would go down to the Arms and get drunk ... (S 338)

> And down in Blawearie next day, what with cooking and chaving and tending to beasts, and wrestling with the worry of the barn, it wasn't half spruced for the dance, Chris might well have gone off her head if Chae and Long Rob of the Mill hadn't come dandering up the road in the afternoon, shy-like, bringing their presents. (S 115)

The effect of initial difficulty with *Sunset Song*, followed by delighted continuous reading, is recorded by many who have come to the book for the first time, from many backgrounds: the initial difficulty is absorbing the rhythms and the minimal repetitive vocabulary features (coarse, quean, and so forth) after which the vocabulary seems natural, the interest of incident takes over, and the alien effort disappears. The style is successful still, and must be given a great deal of the credit for this book's continuing success.

There are many features of the book which strike the Scottish reader as Scottish simply because Scottishness may be associated with particular times of year or particular situations, and these are part of the fabric of *Sunset Song*. Like MacDiarmid, Gibbon was enough of a rebel against the Burns Night to shun the temptation to include that Scottish occasion, indeed he guys it wherever possible throughout *A Scots Quair*. Yet one could catalogue many more: the election of a new minister and the community's dour, fierce interest in the personalities rather than the significance of the Church affairs (S 52); Long Rob's fierce working-class anticlericalism and radicalism (S 27); the community spirit which binds Kinraddie at the time of the burning of Peesie's Knapp (S 76–7) and even more typically the slanderous gossip

which follows, once Chae and his family are safe, enquir-
ing whether they started the fire deliberately to make
insurance money (S 81). Chris's neighbourliness to Rob
(S 167) and Ewan's confidences to Chae (S 177) in France
indicate the neighbourliness of Scot to Scot in times of
difficulty, a closeness which Gibbon cleverly uses to good
effect to underline Chris's emotional turmoil when she and
Rob have a brief affair not long before Rob in his turn goes
to be swallowed up in the war (S 175–6). There are other
things wich draw the reader into the community: the hurt
of readjustment after the war, with the madness of Pooty
(S 184), and the turmoil created by Maggie Jean Gordon
trying to start a trade union for the farm workers
(S 186–7), perhaps a more immediate source of horror to
Kinraddie than the distant world war. By the end of *Sunset
Song* the reader is part of the community affairs sufficiently
closely to identify with what seems important to Kinraddie: the coming of the new minister is a big thing to the
town, and choosing him an important and long-lasting
step.

In language, in situation, *Sunset Song* seems at its best
when it draws the reader into Kinraddie. Yet it exists also
to show the end of the way of life of Kinraddie, and to repel
the reader from a picturebook kailyard Kinraddie. There
is some inherent tension in these various desires.

*   *   *

It is here that the character of Chris is seen in full
advantage, for Chris is the moderator of change. We have
stressed her independence, her cool self-possessed nature,
her apparent dourness in fact a mask to cover deep and
repeated hurt. We have shared the novel with her
thoughts, dipping out and in as the narrative is processed
through her mind, then through her hearer's, then through
an impersonal community mind which gives an over-view.
At the opening of the novel, Chris's adolescent feelings
easily ran over into strong spontaneous emotion; by the
end this is much more difficult, and the style has modified

to show her thoughts, and the responses of others, close together to give the reader some opportunity to make his own deductions. Here, for example, is a peasant narrator-figure overhearing a conversation between Chris and the new minister, her future husband in *Cloud Howe*.

> And there near the fire stood Chris herself, and the Reverend Colquohoun was before her, she was looking up into the minister's face and he'd both her hands in his. And *Oh, my dear, maybe the second Chris, maybe the third, but Ewan has the first for ever!* she was saying, whatever she meant by that; and syne as Dave Brown still looked the minister bent down and kissed her, the fool (S 190)

The style here is rich in satiric perception of Dave Brown's inadequacies as a human observer, but it is also stylistically rich in its exact portrayal of the anticlimax at the end: at one moment we feel the experience of Chris's emotion simultaneously, and the next we are distanced sharply by the insensitivity of Dave Brown.

The same apparent lack of consequential logic builds up a mosaic pattern of response throughout. Here is Chris, meeting Ewan for the first time.

> He looked over young for the coarse, dour brute folk said he was, like a wild cat, strong and quick, she half-liked his face and half-hated it, it could surely never have been him that did THAT in the larch wood of Upperhill? But then if you could read every childe's nature in the way he wiped his nose, said Long Rob of the Mill, it would be a fine and easy world to go through.
>
> So she paid him no more heed and was out of the Knapp a minute later . . . (S 75)

Here we follow her barely-excited train of thought, going from Ewan's appearance to his reputation with girls, then

veering to Long Rob's irreverent remark, then losing
interest. The tone is deliberate: wiping noses and this most
important meeting are juxtaposed deliberately to indicate
the quiet flowering of Chris and Ewan's relationship, as
distinct from a first awakening with all the trappings of a
romantic novel.

Indeed the style moves in barely perceptible ways. Chris
is seen more through other people as she learns to control
her emotions: the community which bulks large in its
interests early in the novel (when John Guthrie was alive,
and Chris was out and about in the community more)
fades as the novel proceeds, and the style spends more
time concentrating on Blawearie and the main circle
of characters. There are set-pieces, wedding, funeral, unveiling of war memorial: there are long-continued
descriptions, the coming of the baby, the cycle of the
seasons as Ewan learns to farm Blawearie.

What the style permits is a steady insight into Chris, and
into her community, and (it has been argued) a measure of
involvement in both.

What the reader thus is invited to take part in is a vision
of change expressed in one character, against a backdrop
which makes that change continuously perceivable
through a coherent range of ideas. Chris experiences;
Scotland changes. The war rages unperceived offstage;
Kinraddie will never be the same after. The author has
specific theories and reasons in his mind for the state of
Kinraddie before, and after the war; the reader has
become emotionally committed to Chris, and wishes her
personal story to continue even when the larger story
which her fate symbolises has lost its immediate point.

What the reader is invited to take from this analysis is a
perception that Gibbon's view of Scotland at the time of his
own adolescence and early manhood is one of change—
certainly—but one of *struggle*. Characters in *Sunset Song*
struggle for survival, for self-awareness, for self-expression.
They struggle against systems, sometimes they succeed,

sometimes fail. But the struggle continues, and continues into *Cloud Howe* and *Grey Granite*.

*   *   *

Oh Chris Caledonia, I've married a nation! laughs Robert, Chris's second husband, minister of Segget (S 298). Scotland, of course, did not cease to exist with Robert's sermon at the unveiling of the war memorial; Scotland struggled on into the poverty of the 1920s and 1930s, and was still struggling when the author wrote his trilogy out in Welwyn Garden City.

The remainder of the trilogy maps out certain very clear ideas. *Cloud Howe* extends to the Church the same scrutiny that *Sunset Song* had given to the agrarian society, as shapers of Scotland's self. The agrarian society is destroyed by the war, but not before it leaves a son to tackle future Scottish problems: the Church struggles in vain to find a satisfactory role with Chris Caledonia, who cannot help Robert in that struggle, a lonely and essentially embittered one, the childlessness of this second marriage a bitter symbol.

Grey Granite completes the process, turning to the cities and the dependence on big business and the capitalism which lay behind the Depression 1930s. Ake Ogilvie, Chris's third husband, is a displaced labourer from Segget; a drifter, he drifts into Chris's life and out again leaving behind little love, and no children. It is a depersonalised marriage largely of convenience, his money making possible Chris's keeping of a lodging house, without which she would starve.

Neither *Cloud Howe* nor *Grey Granite* affords to Chris even the limited satisfaction and happiness she received from her marriage to Ewan, before "civilisation" embittered it. With Robert she knows quiet satisfaction, with Ake security; Ewan is a shadow beyond both marriages, and she can never give herself wholeheartedly to either later husband. And yet are we expected to take from this the conclusion that Scotland can only function in an agrarian mode, and that unsatisfactorily in the twentieth century? Certainly critics would argue support for this point of view, pointing to the extraordinary preponderance of rural novels in Scotland, the relative poverty of urban literature. Critics have pointed to the success of *Sunset Song* compared to the much more modest popularity of the remainder of the trilogy and argued that this diminishing scale reflects Scotland's ability to deal with country, but not with town, in her literature.

Certain things have to be said against this view. One is, that in *Cloud Howe* and in *Grey Granite* Gibbon manages to explore political ideas in theory and in practice, which simply would have been laughed at as irrelevances in Kinraddie. Gibbon the devoted Communist would not be happy to depict his Scotland in terms of the emergent trade unions in Kinraddie in 1919; the trade union movement, and the fight to establish a socialist society throughout Britain, would inevitably take its impetus from the towns with the large mills, the centres of population where mass movements were possible. Canny Kinraddie would laugh even as it laughed at Chae the outspoken Socialist, or Long Rob the radical. In Seggett, a larger and less coherent town, dissent was possible; in Duncairn (which despite the author's disclaimer is most plainly Aberdeen) not only possible, but depicted as a crying necessity.

Yet Segget is perhaps the more immediately interesting example. In *Annals of the Parish* Galt had the weavers, newly attracted to Dalmailing, set themselves up a new suburb of low-grade housing where they lived separate from the historically-established town. The resulting tensions affected the minister obviously enough—attenuation of parish life, absence of weavers from a historical churchgoing tradition, erosion of the minister's function in the community—but life went on, many of the new working class had their own religious observations (or replaced them by an intelligent interest in the world outside far surpassing the minister's own) and the community was seen to adjust in the fifty year span of Galt's novel. In more recent times, this division between old residenters and incomers has polarised into a fiercer hostility: in *Gillespie*, the workers are in one district and the rich in another, even in a small towm, and Barbie's spinners are a very despised and exploited addition to the historical community of *The House with the Green Shutters*.

In *Cloud Howe*, the hostility between the spinners and the established members of the Segget community has many effects, but the most immediately important for our discussion is the fact that Robert Colquohoun can no longer act as community spokesman. Publicly avowed a socialist, he has alienated many of his traditional con-gregation who would no longer accept him as spokesman: not sufficiently socialist for the spinners, he is dismissed by many as "Creeping Jesus." All that Robert can do is try to find an acceptable personal position reconciling his social conscience, his responsibility to his parish (for he feels a responsibility, no matter how little his feelings are reciprocated), his family responsibility, and his Christian-ity. The task is impossible: he dies in the pulpit, after Gibbon had toyed with the idea of a grand trial scene where the Established Church of Scotland would have Robert ejected for his political activities.

Chris, married to Robert and living in the Manse, is effectively exiled to the edge of Segget. She can not in any sense be filter for the activities of her community as she was in *Sunset Song*, even if she had felt that kind of interest in Segget, which assuredly she does not. Therefore Gibbon will inevitably be writing a different kind of novel, and the difference is accelerated and exaggerated in *Grey Granite*.

If Chris was on the edge of Segget life, lacking contact with the spinners, sharing neither her husband's Christian-ity nor his political idealism, and struggling to maintain her own independence of character, then she is doubly the outsider in Duncairn, the keeper of lodgings, her days circumscribed by household tasks, her social position so

low that even her lodgers sometimes despise her. In Segget
she did her work as minister's wife coolly, and kept herself
to herself, relying perhaps on her maid for what news of
Segget she failed to have from her husband; in Duncairn
there is almost no-one, even if she cared to try to take in the
great wash of city gossip. Ma Cleghorn is much too sensible
to be interested in gossip, Ewan too immersed in his work
(later his activities as a communist). Chris is too busy by
day, too tired by night. Ake, when he marries her, has little
to do in binding her to his community nor to hers; their
marriage is soul-less, inward-turned, unemphatic. It is
probably a relief to both when Ake emigrates and leaves
Chris free once more.

In these circumstances, we must look to Gibbon for quite
a different kind of novel, and arguably that kind of novel is
one which by its form tries to indicate the changes
overtaking Scotland since the system described in the
closing pages of *Sunset Song*. There, Scotland was on the
edge of change; in *Cloud Howe* change comes at speed, in
Grey Granite change hangs brooding over the depressed city,
snarling round the corner in a feared social revolution
which is hinted at in the closing pages of the trilogy. The
close community of Scotland in Kinraddie has broken up
(Chris, returning, found sheep on Blawearie: there was no
going back) and so the need for a close, community novel
to evoke that experience has gone too.

In its place Gibbon writes two books which reflect the
progressive breakdown of the community, first into the
multiple but still sharply-described conflicting worlds of
Segget, then into the fragments of the big organism which
is Duncairn, each glimpsed only imperfectly as they impinge briefly on the lives of characters who have no hope of
understanding their workings altogether.

Another change we must take account of: in *Sunset Song*
Gibbon, while occasionally indulging in parody (Pooty),
remained largely and embarrassingly true to real-life,
altering enough and retaining some mask of originality,

significantly changing the co-ordinates of directions and
journeys to confuse the reader. In Segget and Duncairn his
intention is quite different: there are real-life originals
again, but increasingly those features of Scotland which
are attacked are pilloried through gross travesty.

The Mowat family is a case very much in point. In
Kinraddie the members of the upper classes do not impinge
on Chris's life at all, and there is no need to describe them.
In *Cloud Howe* the mill-owners are there to be described,
since Robert wishes to mix with that class and convince
them of the necessity for change. In *Grey Granite* there is no
need to depict the upper classes, but the author chooses to
do so occasionally to give some indication of their responses
to incident and character.

In both later novels, these encounters with higher social
classes are throughout parodied. The Mowat family in its
excess, its immoral leeching of profits from the mill to
sustain a life of private extravagance—the Reverend
MacShilluck in his amoral posturings, his affair with his
housekeeper—the provost with his guilty past—all are
incredible, all no doubt with a seed of fact somewhere but
cruelly blown up compared with the sustaining foreground
of credible characterisation based on Chris. Thus there is a
failure of the struggle in Chris to adjust, to adapt towards
others when she saw the necessity: instead Chris draws in
more and more, and the world develops outside her, the
novelist not allowing her to interact. Even at a lower level,
religion is parodied in Segget in Robert's parishioners, in
the evangelism among the spinners, in Robert's essentially
hopeless dream to bring socially just religion to Scotland.

> *Religion?—A Scot know religion? Half of them think of God*
> *as a Scot with brosy morals and a penchant for Burns. And the*
> *other half are over damned mean to allow the Almighty even*
> *existence.* (S 295)

Chris no longer cares: she has moved away from serious
personal religious belief, and so has young Ewan. In

Duncairn Churchgoing falls away as big city habits replace country ones; only little Miss Murgatroyd, a gross parody, remains with her pottering Episcopalianism, along with the distant MacShilluck preaching to his comfortable congregation.

No, Chris is forced into isolation by the changing kind of novel which Gibbon is trying to write. Chris stands by, a spectator, while Robert tries to convert Segget: she is powerless to help him much of the time, and lacks the will to do more than sustain the home, and help Ewan in his growing. In Duncairn the isolation of the big unfamiliar city adds to the strain of the lodgings, and it is inevitable that apart from Ewan and Ma, and occasional excursions, Chris should lead the most solitary existence. Ake, we have noticed, is no help here.

The sustaining features of community which helped Chris define herself in Kinraddie do not help in Segget: the Church she knows from inside, and the schoolmaster (again an echo from Brown) is an embittered cynic whose advice to Robert is

> *Don't be a fool, leave the swine to stew in their juice*—by swine he meant his fellow-folk of Segget. (S 239)

In Duncairn, she seeks neither minister nor school-master, but (apparently in common with most of her circle) looks to herself. Robert's dream was that "... *men must change, or perish here in Segget, as all over the world*" (S 230–1) but Robert's dream would not come true, at least in Segget in the 1920s.

Chris's isolation is reinforced by her new frankness on the subject to those she no longer fears to offend. She tells Mowat straight that

> *I've been to Dunnottar Castle and seen there the ways that the gentry once liked to keep order. If it came to the push between you and the spinners I think I would give the spinners my vote.* (S 275)

Chris Caledonia here may be expressing disenchantment with the ruling classes, but neither she nor her class has yet found an adequate alternative to the Mowats.

> And the winter was coming. Down in Old Toun a weary indifference lay on the wynds, they paid no heed to the new Election, Chris herself didn't bother to vote—were the liars and cheats called Labour or Tory they'd feather their own nests and lie to the end. (S 340)

The contrasts to Kinraddie's political hustings are obvious. But even this may be better than Duncairn where interest groups, entrenched against each other, simply profit from the occasion. The Provost and Ake bargain to pervert justice to let Ewan off in court (S 455), Jim Trease exploits all events "for their own ends first, not Ewan's" (S 454), the need of the Communist party coming before individual, Ellen Johns tries to tread a difficult path between job and political loyalty, Miss Lyon respects no-one, lives a purely materialistic existence, Mr Piddle amorally gathers news for the papers, seeking only payment—the vision of life in Duncairn is one of fragmentisation, no moral centre or at least none visible from Chris's lodging house.

In *Grey Granite*, Gibbon has created a new kind of world-picture, one quite different from that of *Sunset Song*, so different as to make the critic compare the two with caution. *Grey Granite* is shorter, less coherent, enigmatic, apparently a series of unconnected fragments. Two main things must be emphasised.

One is that *Grey Granite* is attempting to mirror the incoherencies of city life; perceived by Chris, it *is* incoherent, and there is no single village intelligence as there was in Kinraddie to interpret and combine the various fragmentary sub-plots. This is missing in the city—the novel truthfully reflects this apparent incoherence. Alienation is a likely, indeed inevitable consequence which overtakes most of the characters of *Grey Granite*, stranded in an unlovely city in the Depression, shorn of ideals, and with no political or idealistic goal.

The other major difference is that in *Sunset Song* and *Cloud Howe*, the novels had to end with some re-integration of personality and resolution of conflict in Chris, to prepare for the next part of the design of the trilogy. *Grey Granite* has no such demands to put on the novelist. *Grey Granite* in fact divides more than it reconciles, pushing Ewan in one direction at the end, his mother in the opposite. The struggle which is reconciled or temporarily averted at the end of the two previous novels is triumphantly asserted at the end of *Grey Granite*, automatically making any attempt to judge it by the standards of the others almost impossible.

The variable in the argument is the character of young Ewan, now a young man, politically active, independent of home, mother, Church, education—even Scottishness—and experiencing in city life, in involvement with Gowan's and Gloag's the engineering works, the emergence of a political identity, forged in conjunction with the local Communist party, yet responding to his own ideals, and enabling him to plan for a juster future in keeping with his author's views.

Young Ewan remains to be investigated. Then *Grey Granite*, indeed the trilogy, can be finally judged.

*   *   *

Young Ewan learns his mother's self-possession early, when he shrinks from his father returning drunk from the Lanark training camp (S 170), when he learns to adjust to a stepfather with unnatural speed (S 206). He naturally enough asks Robert in *Cloud Howe* about Jesus, and is told that Jesus is "our Father and Mother, our End and Beginning": equally naturally,

> Ewan's eyes would open wider at that. *My mother's here and my father's dead.* Robert would laugh and upset his chair, *A natural sceptic . . .* (S 206)

He is brought up to amuse himself (like his creator with books, with flints, with archaeology) and to think for himself: he outrages Segget ideas on well-brought-up children, but he pleases his mother by his independence of thought (S 270). Interestingly, in part III of *Cloud Howe* Gibbon begins the process of investing the reader with the thoughts of Ewan's mind as well as of Chris's, as Ewan grows old enough to be interesting to the reader. The process is skilfully enough done, through adolescent bewilderment to the same façade of precocious calm that Chris Guthrie had learned in the earlier novel: there is the same memory of childhood adolescent fumbling with questions of sex that haunted Malcom Maudslay in *The Thirteenth Disciple*, with Charlie Cronin the young working-class boy Ewan was friendly with.

> Charlie Cronin drew pictures in the lavatories at school, the silly ass couldn't draw at all. So you drew some yourself to show how things were, he turned red-faced when you drew IT so well. *Ewan, that's dirty!* What was dirty about it? (S 277)

Ewan treats his mother with a little less reserve, but the barriers are always up. To himself, he calls her Chris: "She didn't know that you called her that, to yourself, not aloud, aloud you said *Mother*. But Robert, just *Robert*, he wasn't your father . . ." (S 278)

What Gibbon is doing is giving Ewan his own version, in *Cloud Howe*, of the Scottish Chris/English Chris tug in *Sunset Song*. Ewan's self-possession is expressed, as Chris's was, in Englishness: he rejects

> . . . the poetry of Burns, silly Scotch muck about cottars and women, and love and dove and rot of that sort . . . Poetry was rot, why not say it plain, when a man kissed a woman or a woman had a baby? (S 280)

The cool self-possession Ewan displays angers Segget, and perceiving this anger through Ewan's young mind is a

cleverly-observed process. But then Ewan can observe
anger because he feels very little, for Chris even, certainly
for Robert and his friend John Cronin. Chris even tries to
shock him out of this self-possession:

> *Oh Ewan, you're hard and cool as—grey granite! When you
> too grow up you'll find facts over much—you'll need something
> to follow that's far from the facts.* (S 283)

But then this is Chris the mother speaking, and she has not
yet had the hurt of losing her second, idealist husband.
"Well you saw nothing to make you excited, except now
and then a broad-flake flint."

Ewan does grow up, and indeed emotion touches him
occasionally, particularly when he thinks Chris is dying.
"But he did it only a minute while she held him, then drew
away and took out his handkerchief and wiped his eyes,
and sat down, calm . . . him no longer a baby, remote from
her thoughts or from thought of her. How nearer he was
than any there were!" (S 308–9). They have the bond of
shared experience from the previous novel: it is Ewan who
has the courage to tell Chris of her lost baby in *Cloud Howe*,
and she can take the bad news from him.

Adolescence brings Ewan out into public notice, and
into a passion for flints and all amateur archaeology: there
is a curious description of him by the Segget voice, probably an echo of the author's own reception in Arbuthnott.

> Charming and cool, a queer-like loon, not right in the
> head, folk that were nice weren't near so polite.
> (S 315)

But then even Chris has this treatment from her son most
of the time—he has perfected his defence mechanisms
against the world.

> He never went by with a loon-like slouch, or reddened
> up, loon-like, over the lugs, if he met with a covey of
> queans in the Square—damn't, there was something

unnatural about him, a sly young brute, you could well believe. And what though they said he did well at college? No doubt his stepfather, the minister Colquohoun, did all his lessons and he got the credit. (S 335)

Girls try to lead him on, but he rebuffs them: even Ag Moultrie, the memorable Roarer and Greeter of Segget gossip fame, is no match for him.

What Ewan is touched by (apart from some feeling for Chris) is not the here and now of Segget—for Gibbon cannot make Ewan (who belongs to *Grey Granite*) too involved with Segget—but the concerns of a wider social problem which barely impinges on Segget, certainly not on the Manse and the social circle which frequent it. His school chum Cronin from the weavers' village, and Cronin's father, tell Ewan something of the conditions down there, and Ewan is moved to physical sickness by what he hears: "He was turning to look in the face of Life", Gibbon records (S 342) and the process is abruptly accelerated when Robert Colquohoun dies in the pulpit, preaching a Christian, but socially just, future,

> *a stark, sure creed that will cut like a knife, a surgeon's knife through the doubt and disease—men with unclouded eyes may yet find it, and far off yet in the times to be . . .* (S 350)

Now Chris and Ewan are marooned to face the financial uncertainties of *Grey Granite*.

In *Grey Granite* Ewan shares the limelight with his mother so it is right that he should receive a good deal of attention throughout, rather than the sporadic clumps of description adequate in the preceding work. At the outset, he rejects the easy path of the Manse and the minister's son—he refuses to go to college (University) when his mother can hardly afford it. Already he has responded to Robert's death by adopting a protective attitude to his mother: as she prophesied, he has had to find something

beyond facts, and he has found in it emotional commitment to his mother. He expresses that commitment in
finding himself a job, an apprentice in Gowans and Gload,
ironsmelters.

> ... *But, Ewan, you'd go daft in a job like that.* He said he'd
> try not to, awfully hard, especially as it was the best
> job he could come by—*and I can come out in week-ends
> and see you quite often. Duncairn's only a twenty miles off.*
> (S 359)

Naturally, Chris elects to move to Duncairn, and so the
stage is set for a novel which looks at Aberdeen and the
kind of fragmented experience which it has been suggested
is necessary to round out Gibbon's picture of Scotland,
after the farming village and the small town. But the
initiative is moving away from Chris: Ewan found the job
and decided to move to the city without even consulting
her.

Ewan adjusts to the city remarkably, "no fancies or flim-
flams with Ewan at all" (S 363): the work of the furnaces is
challenging physically (and therefore exciting) and
stimulating mentally, and Ewan's self-possession learned
in Segget stands him in good stead, making him resistant to
the unpleasantness of the work, and the hostility of the
working-class labourers his own age who resent his
apprentice status and his book learning. "The other
apprentices, keelies the lot, didn't seem anxious to chum
up at all, thank goodness ..." (S 372) and in this initial
part of the novel Ewan is able to live out the life of the
English Chris much more than his mother could in the
community of Kinraddie.

Ewan's responses to the lodgers in his mother's house are
typical of his cool detachment, indeed the overstatement of
that very detachment is Gibbon's warning to the reader
that Ewan is not yet a completed character. Gibbon and
Wells we know to have been good personal friends: Gibbon
is hardly allowing Ewan to speak for him when Ewan

dismisses Miss Murgatroyd's generation as one that

> blethered in their books about little else, Shaw and the
> little sham-scientist Wells running a fornication a folio
> before they could pitch an idea across: gluey devils,
> the Edwardians, chokers and chignons, worse than
> the padded Victorian rabbits ... (S 378)

If he rejects her politics, he rejects her faded Scottishness
too, her advocacy of Pittendrigh MacGillivray and Miss
Marion Angus, *"though they're awful broad"*—but such a
ridiculous statement cannot move a Ewan who is simply
not interested. Ewan reads neither novels nor poetry;
books on castings and metallurgy occupy his imaginative
life adequately at this stage.

Two things move Ewan out of this into manhood. One is
Ellen Johns, the other a mature political commitment to a
wider society.

Ellen Johns, Chris's new lodger, introduces Ewan to
socialism, and breaks into his intense self-possession. Ewan
begins their relationship not caring about politics or social
justice or a better era: *"It won't come in our time. I've my own
life to lead"*. He won't allow others to dictate his political
creed. *"They won't rule me. I'm myself"* (S 387). But he
agrees, under the influence of Ellen's attraction, to look
into politics, and he takes from her criticism he would
never have accepted from a less pretty critic: *". . . Don't
be so horribly superior: you'll never lead if you can't be an equal"*
(S 388). The direct consequence of this is Ewan's involvement with the keelies, with his colleagues at work. He takes
an interest in a life outside his own, he becomes involved,
he understands the working classes as human beings. It is
quite a new idea for him.

The second thing is a direct consequence: mixing more
with others, Ewan is thrown into a political demonstration
which he encounters—significantly enough, while leaving
a bookshop. The real world outside the shop is one of
marchers and police, communist organisers and genuinely

poor and starving men protesting. The parodied stock
responses of the middle- and upper-class citizens briefly
reported are contrasted to the reality of hunger and
marching and police brutality, and Ewan feels genuine
anger. This is true involvement for him at last, and it is a
turning point in the book.

Ewan taken time to adjust, and he draws into his
protective shell while he thinks things through, being rude
even to good-hearted Ma Cleghorn,

> ... the old fool should heed to her own damned
> business. Chris looked at you with her nice, cool eyes,
> a long time since you'd kissed her, she had a nice kiss.
> Then you went up the stairs to your flints. (S 406)

Ewan would not have responded so violently before, nor
would he have allowed his response to show. Now he is
feeling enough real anger to break his self-possession and
drive him back into himself to find out what is really in his
mind.

What is in his mind is organised socialism, the organising
of trade unions in the works (to the danger of his job for
he is immediately threatened with victimisation by the
management), the organising of the working classes to
support the union. In this Ewan is supported by Ellen, like
himself someone not afraid of public ridicule, and the two
of them are for a while colleagues in their struggle to set up
a socialist movement. Ellen acutely sees that Ewan's heart
is less in the struggle than his head and imagination
(S 414), but Ewan has now the maturity to see the struggle
will take time, at history's own pace, and that no human
impatience will help. In this he is allied to the communist
organiser Jim Trease, calm, unhurried, surviving endless
rebuffs and setbacks; Ewan, too, sees the magnitude of the
problem and accepts that he may not live to see the
consequences—yet refuses to give up the struggle just
because of that.

For Ewan the climax comes when at a New Year dance

for his Young League branch, he sees his lifetime commitment to the cause of social justice. He can no longer
keep apart, for he sees that the working classes—the
keelies—are his responsibility much as he would like to
keep his apartness:

> the blood and bones and flesh of them all, their
> thoughts and their doubts and their loves were his, all
> that they thought and lived in were his. And that
> Ewan Tavendale that once had been, the cool boy
> with the haughty soul and cool hands, apart and
> alone, self-reliant, self-centred, slipped away out of
> the room as he stared, slipped away and was lost
> from his life forever. (S 430)

In counterpoint to this are the episodes where he is captured and beaten up by the police, when he and Ellen first
sleep together then discover their physical attraction to one
another (their nightly visits to one another eventually a
scandal to the lodgers). What is interesting is that the
episodes of growing intimacy between Ewan and Ellen are
seen not through Ewan's eyes but through Ellen's for
example in S 472–3. We do not know what Ewan is
thinking in these scenes, though his physical response to
Ellen is the normal one of desire, and he plainly takes
pleasure in the nightly visits. Yet it is Ellen who visits him,
not the reverse. Something is still secret and reserved in
Ewan, whatever he thought at that New Year's Day
dance. Chris, whose affairs are complex enough at this time
(with the death of Ma, the buying of the lodgings, her
marriage to Ake) is perceptive enough to see what is
missing in the relationship:

> Ewan looked at the two cool and frank, amused and a
> little bored, as he might at a friend who played with a
> kitten ...
> And Chris thought, appalled, *Poor Ellen, poor Ellen!*
> (S 478)

It is altogether typical of Chris that she does not try to interfere in their relationship: like his mother, Ewan has to make his own mistakes and learn from his own hurts, even though he may hurt others. His involvement is increasingly with Trease and with organising the cells of the Communist party: the political involvement Gibbon might have undertaken had he remained in Aberdeen and continued his youthful communism into manhood. Selden's defection with the Party's money hurts him because of the work it renders impossible: Ewan seems less hurt by Ellen's defection. After a night spent sleeping with her, he tackles her on her disaffiliation from the Communist Party.

In the confrontation Ewan has to make a choice between Ellen, and his party; he also has to make a choice between her common-sense view of his struggle, and his own idealistic vision of it. Ellen left the Communists because of party weakness,

> ... *I'm sick of it, full of cheats and liars, thieves even, look at Selden, there's not one a clean or a decent person except you and perhaps Jim Trease. And I've left because I'm sick of being without decent clothes, without the money I earn myself, pretty things that are mine, that I've worked for ... Oh, Ewan, you know they're hopeless, these people—the keelies remember you used to call them?—hopeless and filthy; if ever there's anything done for them it'll be done from above, not by losing oneself in them ...* (S 490)

She has left also because membership would have cost her her job; she is victimised too like Ewan, but while Ewan is content to lose his job, Ellen (perhaps because she is a woman, vulnerable like the English Chris) hangs on to what she has gained in her society, and tries to explain to Ewan why she has made the choice she has.

Ewan's response is shocking, to the reader, to Ellen.

> *Go to them then in your comfortable car—your Labour Party and your comfortable flat. But what are you doing out here with me? I could get a prostitute anywhere.*

With that, Ewan walks away from Ellen, finally. He has cut her out of his life, apparently without regret. It is part of the new composite personality he adopts as a Communist worker: his loyalties seem to be to no one, not even to Jim Trease as the book speeds to a fragmentary close and Ewan is off to London to work for the Communist party there:

> ... they shook hands, liking each other well, nothing to each other, soldiers who met a moment at night under the walls of a town yet unstormed. (S 493)

His mother's son is described there: when Chris is breaking up her lodgings, Ake having left her, she realises that Archie Clearmont one of her lodgers has secretly loved her for years,

> And Chris had known and smiled, known what he wanted, and kissed him, and watched him go striding away, and thought, kind, *Nice boy*; and forgotten him. (S 494)

Ewan's unnatural self-possession and emotional barriers are quite explicable in terms of his mother's character.

Yet even at the last stages of the novel Gibbon is careful to bring Chris and Ewan back together for comparison, to ask what Ewan is leaving behind in leaving Scotland and the world of the Scottish Chris, for the world which the English Chris would gladly have gone to in *Sunset Song* had her birth and her upbringing allowed her. Ewan shows a flash of nostalgia:

> ... the hard young keelie with the iron jaw softening a moment to a moment's memory: *Do you mind Segget Manse and the lawn in Spring?*
> Chris said that she minded, and smiled upon him, in pity, seeing a moment how it shook him, she herself beyond such quavers ever again. (S 495)

And in that last evening together mother and son exchange confidences, as never before and never again.

> *The world's sought faith for thousands of years and found only death or unease in them. Yours is just another dark cloud to me—or a great rock you're trying to push up a hill.*

He said it was the rock was pushing him; and sat dreaming again . . . all those to-morrows that awaited his feet by years and tracks Chris would never see, dropping the jargons and shields of his creed, thinking again as once when a boy, openly and honestly, kindly and wise:

> *There will always be a you and I, I think, Mother. It's the old fight that maybe will never have a finish, whatever the names we give to it—the fight in the end between FREEDOM and GOD.* (S 495)

Again we are in the world of the essay "Religion" in *Scottish Scene*: "One sees rise ultimately . . . in place of Religion—Nothing". That will remain when religion passes, given the natural benevolence of Man: yet Gibbon goes further. "Men are not merely the victims, the hapless leaves storm-blown, of historic forces, but may guide if they cannot generate that storm . . ." (ScS 326). Ewan, on the edge of hunger march, and hoped-for Communist revolution, knows he cannot control that storm, but he is prepared to sacrifice his career and his home to guiding the storm; Chris is not.

This polarisation is the ultimate position achieved in *A Scots Quair*. Young Ewan marches off to London in the closing pages, and Chris (her third marriage broken up and her life in Aberdeen finished) returns—but not to Kinraddie, where civilisation buffetted her sorely, rather to the Aberdeenshire of her ancestors, and there the trilogy ends on a quite extraordinary note of enigma.

The final Chris is a woman of the country, "concerning none and concerned with none", returning to the outward condition of the peasant, working the land, refusing

commitment, seeing "only the land, enduring, encompass-
ing". What she has learned to accept is Change, "whose
right hand was Death and whose left hand Life",
"Deliverer, Destroyer and Friend in one". Time she went
home, she thinks musing,

> But she still sat on as one by one the lights went out
> and the rain came beating the stones about her, and
> falling all that night while she still sat there, presently
> feeling no longer the touch of the rain or hearing the
> sound of the lapwings going by. (S 496)

What is going on here? Perhaps Chris is sitting into the
dark to symbolise her complete union with the land,
making herself uncaring of dark and cold and wet. Perhaps
she is fading into the land, some representation of her
ceasing to exist in a merely material plain. Perhaps she is
dying, like Mrs Yeobright in *The Return of the Native* or The
Philosopher in Neil Gunn's *The Serpent*, dying so im-
perceptibly that she seems an unmoving fixture on the land
with which she is identified, till bystanders find her body.

Yet it is entirely in keeping with the trilogy as we have
analysed it that it should end in enigma.

The Land, unchanging, influencing and little influenced, has survived. Chris seems inevitably to be moved
away from the Land to the small town to the city, but she
returns to the Land which claimed her loyalty as Scottish
Chris over the cultural affiliations of her society, and over
English Chris. Her civilisation which seemed to encompass
her and thwart her development, to take away her first
husband and her happiness in Kinraddie, thwart her
second husband and make him kill himself with overwork,
thrust her into a deadly environment and a sterile
marriage in the third novel, this civilisation has lost; Chris
is still free and independent at the end, still able to claim
her freedom from creed. She sees the necessity for Change
against the stable backdrop of The Land: she is hurt, but

she learns adaptation and survival mechanisms. As a person she has survived.

Finally, her Scottishness survives. Although there is less in Segget that seems essentially or naturally Scotland, and still less in Duncairn, the "alien effort" of being Scottish never overwhelms Chris's natural ability to express herself, to think things through for herself, to articulate what she wishes through her veil of self-possession. She is not interested in Scottish culture or literature because she is not interested in culture or literature: she survives, she gets through each day and insofar as she represents the Scottish people (which plainly Chris Caledonia must do by the end of the trilogy) she must in part be a statement about the possibilities of Scottishness in the here and now of Gibbon's Scotland—a continuing identity more in class struggle, and survival against hostile and ugly invasions of alien effort, than in the visible signs of Scottishness in dress, accent, speech, literature, customs. Chris returns to the anonymity of the life of a Scottish peasant as the widow Ogilvie. For her, survival and Scottishness are un-emphatic, bound to the very last paragraph with the permanent features of The Land.

For Ewan, the opposite conditions seem to prevail. Ewan progressively sheds the Scottish features which matter to his mother, he sheds the wish to live on the land, to identify with any community linked to the values of the land, to stay even in Scotland, let alone Aberdeenshire. Ewan has come to terms with the land, by ignoring it save in moments of reminiscence which are uncharacteristic, if effective through their unexpectedness. Ewan has come to terms with civilisation, by fiercely engaging in the struggle to shape the storms of an evolving society changing rapidly in postwar depression, moving towards a Communist revolution which will overturn the rottenness of the social fabric of Duncairn, and by implication Segget and Kinraddie. But Ewan does not care: civilisation has so undone those communities that their loss does not seriously touch him, any more than Ellen's loss seems to. Ewan has come to terms with Scottishness, by never letting it enter very seriously into his decision-making or discussion. Ewan does not show the slightest interest in the signs by which an average Scot signifies his cultural loyalty, in literature or song or language: Ewan rejects it all, and turns to the timeless and international activities of archaeology, politics, social organisation, struggle. These seem for him to bulk larger and more important than nationalist politics, literature, cultural survival. The poverty of Duncairn makes the twitterings of Miss Murgatroyd's anaemic Scottishness ridiculous—not that Gibbon ever gives the Scottish nationalist renaissance writers much of a chance, for they are pilloried throughout. The reader can hardly avoid a cultural identification with Ewan in his disgust.

Yet neither Chris nor Ewan seriously acts against what we could reasonably expect of them by the end of the trilogy. Chris makes her cultural commitment to the land in *Sunset Song*, and in returning to the land at the end of *Grey Granite* she reaffirms the emergence of the Scottish Chris, modified by the rarely-seen third Chris who kept her other two selves in line after her maturity. In refusing political commitment she is entirely in keeping with her early background of Scottish peasant independence. In refusing to leave Scotland even to do something about the social evils of the 1930s she is quite in keeping with the settled, middle-aged, thrice-married matron she is becoming, despite her attractive looks. Chris could not reasonably be asked to join Ewan, any more than he shows any interest in asking her to.

Ewan, on the other hand, could not reasonably be asked to stay in a country he treats with total indifference, when the lure of London with its opportunities and its social challenges is so near and the need so desperate. Nor can we be surprised that he is prepared eventually to sacrifice his relationship even with Ellen for his intellectualised

commitment to Communism. His rejection of her is sudden
and brutal, but nothing in the book (other than the
author's statement that at a New Year dance the cool,
remote Ewan walked out of his life for ever) prepares us
to accept a more rounded character capable of serious
commitment to another, nor indeed capable of compassion
on a large scale. Ewan's commitment is to change, to
organisation, to creating revolution. Ewan's rejection of
Ellen is a sacrifice made so quickly as to suggest the total
subjection of his natural physical desires to his overwhelm-
ing mental control.

Ellen's affair with Ewan is a welcome affirmation of
Ewan's normality, for he is in danger of being a purely
abstract character, so deadly earnest and consistent is his
behaviour throughout. But Ellen is herself an enigma: she
is the English Chris who actually tries to bridge the
cultural divide, and fails. Does this mean that there is no
bridge between the English character and the Scottish?
Gibbon leaves this question also unanswered: the separation between Chris and Ewan certainly suggests a gulf
which will not easily be crossed.

It is in the consideration of that gulf that we return,
finally, to that phrase in the minister's address at the war
memorial in *Sunset Song*, that phrase which sticks in the
memory. In the future, he fears, Scotland will only be
expressed with "alien effort": has Gibbon himself been
reduced to alien effort in the schematisation of *A Scots
Quair*?

A critic could point to the extreme sketchiness of the end
of *Grey Granite*, the falling-apart of strands of plot, the
hustling of Ake Ogilvie overseas (as quickly as previous
husbands had been disposed of). Gibbon has set Chris and
Ewan apart in unnatural contrast to show the cultural
extremes of Scotland and England. He has forced
apartness on them. They are like Davie Balfour and Alan
Breck, necessary to each other yet forced at the end of
Catriona to part by a Stevenson who saw in their two

characters the two sides of Scotland, irreconcilable in the conditions of modern life.

Positively, one might point to the entire consistency of character which brings Chris to Benachie, Ewan to the London road on the march for social equality. They do what is entirely predictable, and if they show a lack of visible emotion it can be credited to their natural reserve, and to the tribulations of a hectic plot which have taught them reserve.

Gibbon shows two possible solutions, the two sides of Scottish character externalised in two perfectly credible and successful characters: two solutions, one the emigrant to London, the other the stay-at-home. If Stevenson in *Catriona* and *The Master of Ballantrae* did the same he solved the impasse by emigration of one part, or death of both: Gibbon shows a compartmentalisation to make struggle possible on one side, and acceptance in the other. And plainly he believes in both.

Our analysis throughout has shown Gibbon's belief in struggle, in the necessity to fight against civilisation and the degradation of Depression Britain. That struggle requires the character of a Ewan, a character Gibbon plainly sees as part of the modern Scot. Gibbon equally stresses the need for an emotional basis to life, the Land part of the Scottish Chris's character, and the supremacy that part is likely to have in the mind of any Scot, quite unconsciously and independent of cultural forces from family or education. Chris, too, is part of the modern Scot.

But can the modern Scot live with these irreconcilables? This is the question which *A Scots Quair* does not finally answer. In "Literary Lights" the predicament of the modern Scottish author was described but not resolved: Gibbon's own style was mentioned as a brilliant possibility towards avoiding "alien effort". Yet there, the irreconcilables continue, while in *A Scots Quair* the irreconcilables seem finally separated, the tension removed. Chris can return to her roots on the enigmatic last page, Ewan can leave for the future as he sees it in the struggles of a wider political arena. The tension is now a quite different one, much less a Scottish one.

Thus the critic is faced with a difficulty. The style, we have argued, is chosen and cultivated to make possible the gradual mutation of view which is attributed to Chris as the trilogy matures. That *Grey Granite* should end in a way very different from *Sunset Song* is quite in keeping with this feature of its author's work. Rather, an author who saw life as struggle, has partially removed the struggle in his character at the end of the trilogy by the separation of Chris from her son, Scotland from England as political arenas, the city from the country. In life, such separation could hardly take place beyond the pages of the kailyard. What is the effect of the separation in fiction? Should we judge the fiction against life? This must be the question of our final chapter.

CHAPTER VI

SOME CONCLUSIONS

Grassic Gibbon has given recent critics of Scottish fiction
some difficulty in coming to terms with his "great but
overworked talent" (Maurice Lindsay), his taking part in
what Francis Hart has described as

> ... the assumption that cultural survival is doomed or
> unlikely, and that the novelist must stridently resist
> the inevitable, meet it with polemic, or compensate
> for it with elegaic urgency.

Gibbon hardly fits into the pattern Professor Hart wishes
for, a novelist who could write "with a measure of ease"
about the problems of his society. For one thing he had not
the time, and in *The Speak of the Mearns* (probably written
very late in his career) he was still writing about the past,
about his schooling, about the cultural conflict plainly
surrounding his own childhood, rather than drawing back
for an overview. For Gibbon, the urgency of the Scottish
Scene was in the close-up of the mind of the person living
through the Scottish Scene, working the land, taking in the
harvest, seeing the world through his own distorted
spectacles, when

> ... a man had time to sit down with his paper and
> read of the Irish Catholics, the dirt, them that wanted
> Home Rule and the like silly fairlies, the foul ungodly
> brutes that they were. (SoM 73)

The irony is lost on the farmer himself, as is the dirt of his
community, the cultural dereliction and the calls for Home
Rule in Scotland. Gibbon's great, overworked talent only

had time to mature in this ironic mode and its most conspicuous success—*Sunset Song*, has been where the ironic view was narrowest, where the observing intelligences were most narrow and myopic, and where the identification of the reader was with the narrowest and most inflexible of communities—Kinraddie. As the ironic perspective of Gibbon's analysis of Scotland widened, to Segget and to Duncairn, the impact of his trilogy weakened and it has taken years of patient critical explication to rescue the later novels from some suspicion that they were written in haste, poor in construction and somehow less meritorious than the warm, welcoming Kinraddie of *Sunset Song*. Small wonder that Gibbon felt impelled to go back to the small and the rural for *The Speak of the Mearns*, to the Kinneff of his childhood rambles and Maiden Castle whose ruins he must often have explored on his bicycle rides from Arbuthnott. As Keith Stratoun grew and matured in *The Speak of the Mearns*, we must assume his perspective would have widened, the ironic distance between his widening vision and the hectic sexual scandals of the Howe (detailed in the author's notes) growing more and more insistent, and Gibbon playing the familiar balancing game between identification with the warm community, and revulsion from its narrow standards.

That he had a flexible scale is now quite evident, that he could evoke the strands of response from his readers' views on the land, on their civilisation, on their Scottishness real or sympathetic—our lengthy analysis of *A Scots Quair* has taken as its central motif the need to draw away from a simple identification as a critical criterion of excellence, but to look for something more complex in the developing characters and the developing trilogy. We have seen the shift of emphasis from Chris as perceiver and interpreter to the more complex double and multiple perspectives of Duncairn, via the breaking-down in Segget; we have discussed at the end of the preceding chapter the ways in which the gradual dissolution of a single, unitary

viewpoint removes from the reader the easy sympathetic identification which gave pleasure—intentional
pleasure—to the reading of *Sunset Song*, but which had no
place at the end of the novel in 1919, still less in the Segget
of the 1920s and the Duncairn of the 1930s at the worst
point of the Depression. Inasmuch as Gibbon is using
multiple viewpoints to show an ironically mixed view of his
country and his countrymen, in the wider context of a
cultural and political map of Great Britain, then simple
identification with Kinraddie is indeed an outworn and
unworthy criterion. We may guess that identification with
the Howe would not long have satisfied Keith Stratoun in
The Speak of the Mearns, any more than Malcom Maudslay
or Thea Mayven can remain content for long with the
powerful and genuine identifications of their earliest years.
The experience of living as Gibbon sees it and puts it in his
novels is to wrench the emerging sensibility and the
emerging intellect from that early frame, and force on
them wider and wider frames, and in the process force the
making of comparisons, ironic or regretful, between the
complex now and the easier past.

The "alien effort" of the reader of the 1920s and 1930s
looking back on Kinraddie before the War is obviously
much amplified in the 1980s, whether through the realised
visual medium of television (which has had an impact on
the book's sales still hard to quantify as these words are
written) or the written word which continues to make
increasing impact on the readers who buy the easily
available paperback editions for school and university use,
and for pleasure reading. Alien effort indeed for a
generation to whom Arbuthnott in 1911 is a vanished
world, and for whom the mental assumptions necessary to
be a part of that Arbuthnott are almost impossible to
imagine. Gibbon wrote from suburban Welwyn Garden
City, from a comfortable brick house with garage and
motor car, radio and electricity, of a world of bothies and
primitive conditions he was already having to recreate

with effort; still more so half a century later, the majority of
his readers turn to the essays on " The Land" for the
necessary emotional and intellectual stimulus to re-live
those conditions in their full discomfort, not be merely
sidetracked by the beauty of the peewits, the harvest
madness, the astringent attractions of life in the Mearns.
Gibbon himself found an ambivalent pleasure in returning
to that life, even in his motor car for brief family holidays.
Today the imagination revisits those scenes with greater
difficulty.

Hence the stress throughout these pages on the ironic
multiple readings of reality, remembered and actual, made
possible by Gibbon's manipulation of viewpoint as Chris
changes, as her husbands' ideas interplay with hers, as
Ewan comes finally to interpose his ideas between her and
her reader at the end of *Grey Granite*. If Professor Hart
regrets that "a measure of ease" cannot be found in writing
about the contemporary in Scotland, Gibbon's reply
might have been to point to the extremity of the problem,
the social ills in the country as well as the city, the
vanishing cultural inheritance and the fraudulence of
much that seeks to preserve it in the name of Scottish
culture and literature. Hence the "polemic", the "elegaic
urgency" of *A Scots Quair*. It is not the urgency of
preservation before it is too late, for there is a clear sense at
the conclusion of *Sunset Song* that Robert Colquohoun is
right when he unveils the monument—that Kinraddie is
dead with Long Rob and with Chae and with Ewan
Tavendale, just as surely as it died with the cutting of the
trees and the dividing up of the farms into great
mechanised agglomerations without the bothies and the
families who made up the backbone of Kinraddie. To go
back to that would be alien effort, it would be knowingly
artificial and it would be impossible—it would lead to the
twitterings of a Miss Murgatroyd, the sour alienation of a
Mr Geddes from Segget in *Cloud Howe*. Rather the polemic
and the elegaic urgency of Gibbon's *Quair* come from the

need to see the present clearly, with the sudden devastating clarity of Chris and Ewan the night before they split up at the end of *Grey Granite*, the clarity which forces Ewan to political action, and Chris to face up to the great Change which has haunted her, half-perceived but never acknowledged, all her life. It is at the same time painful and honest, and it hardly makes for easy or unstressed writing.

Not for Gibbon the easy popularity of Miss Murgatroyd's favourites. "Mr Gibbon must surely confess the distortion to his own heart", wrote *The Scotsman*; the *Kirriemuir Free Press*, recalling that the kailyard "gave us pictures of Scottish life at its best", regretted that realistic fiction today tends "to gloat foully". The *Paisley Express* came right to the point.

> The unredeemed close-packed filth, meanness, spite, brutality, lying squalor and stupidity wearies us. (ScS 208–9).

The author, typically, gathered such reviews gleefully—he carefully filed his reviews, pasted them up in scrapbooks, and wrote to MacDiarmid soliciting brash and unfavourable Scottish press items to spice the pages of *Scottish Scene*, where these critical lambastings of himself were printed mischievously. This is a playful author who quite seriously sets out to offend. Offence is not negative, it shocks but does not repel; rather it draws in, it prepares the reader through content to co-operate with the style, the *parole intérieure*, the closely realised picture of village life and to move from alien effort to a synthesised but natural acceptance of the Scottish setting of *Sunset Song*. The cold-blooded destruction of Kinraddie by the forces around it then offends the reader without Gibbon's polemic, and indeed there is remarkably little polemic in *A Scots Quair* from the author himself. Young Ewan, perhaps, expresses it but then his voice is hardly uncritically his author's. The shape of *Grey Granite*, its half-perceived civic institutions so bitterly failing its citizens at a time of stress, its brutal policemen encountered only as tyrants and repressors, its churchmen and civic personalities travestied, these are no doubt the author's polemic; but the shape of *Grey Granite*, its deliberate lack of a central authorial vision, its fragmented nature and chaotic time-scheme make the polemic visible but non-intrusive. The reader may not agree with the view expressed in *Grey Granite*, but he hardly ascribes it to the author with the ease with which he might ascribe the views of the Scottish Chris in *Sunset Song*. Rather the fragmented view of Duncairn is accepted for its very stressed, fragmented nature as being the best possible in the circumstances to a set of partial observers obsessed with work, with hunger, with political ambition, with the daily worry of running a house, with an emergent personality crisis—there is no central view in *Grey Granite*, and so no alien effort in tailoring the reader's view to that central one. The book's bewilderment catches the reader's expected response, and mirrors it, preparing the reader for the painful end to the trilogy.

There is a clear economy of effort in Gibbon's achievement in *A Scots Quair*. The "Sunset" of *Sunset Song* spelt out the end of a way of life, more clearly than the "scum of kailyard romance" which Gibbon detested in *Scottish Scene*, more clearly still when Chris returns to Kinraddie in *Cloud Howe* and finds only sheep and dereliction where half a generation before there had been a vibrant community. With the cutting of the trees and the thinning of the rural community the Scottish reader is given a clear external indication of the passing of a Scottish way of life rooted in centuries of tradition, the end of the marriage feasts and the singing, the closeness of community and friend and farm. In their place come the more austere and impersonal—and far less Scottish—traditions of Segget, and worst of all of Duncairn. For the Scottish reader, as for Chris who tries to revisit the Blawearie of her youth, there is no going back.

But Gibbon cleverly manipulates his non-Scots reader in

the trilogy, as cleverly as did MacDiarmid in his lyrics. For the experience of reading *Sunset Song* in particular is to be drawn into the Scottish community with the immediacy of one who might imagine himself to have known it personally, the universal situation and character and incident and country setting almost placeless, the easily accessible language characteristics giving a sort of access to the Scottish experience. This experience, too, is rudely ended with the close of *Sunset Song*, and the lesson rubbed home in the remainder of the trilogy. There is no going back to that country once visited—it has gone, despite the kailyard longings. The here and the now of Duncairn is Gibbon's honest transmission of Scottishness, despite his own memories and his own longings, and despite the fact that he found the inspiration to end the trilogy sitting on the top of the Barmekin, surrounded by Scotland's beauty and the remembered scenes of his earliest years. This is not alien effort, but a painful reminder of the survival of the past against the call of reason, the struggle of the instinctive Scottish primitive response against the realisation that it is, essentially, dead.

In sum, Gibbon is an author who appeals on a wide front—for the beauty of his language, for the exactness with which he evokes a vanished and vanishing way of life, for the startling excellence of his characters and the skill with which he controls a substantial plot to follow his characters through *A Scots Quair*. We have noticed at every point that while *A Scots Quair* is the book which brought him to fame and wide recognition, the themes which are entangled in our discussion form part of all his work, and his preoccupations cannot be kept out of his many projects, archaeological, historical, scientific. In time, other books may be reprinted. For the present, he is enjoying a revival of his fortunes as author of *A Scots Quair*, and it is certainly the intention of this analysis to move away from an easy acknowledgment of stylistic virtuosity, and a regret for the passing of Kinraddie. Rather it has been the intention to show *A Scots Quair* as the summation of a long argument of the writer's mind and divided personality; for him, as for Chris and Ewan, the identity of the writer/reader is in the struggle between FREEDOM and GOD, a struggle which continues beyond the book, and far beyond any gratification of memory or stylistic pleasure.

Chris in *Sunset Song*, her father newly dead and her future dizzyingly spread out before her, feels in one pang the ambivalence of her position as she stumbles out into the storm to find and feed the cattle. They

> ... stood in the lithe of the freestone dyke that ebbed and flowed over the shoulder of the long ley field, and ... hugged to it close from the drive of the wind, not heeding her as she came among them, the smell of their bodies foul in her face—foul and known and enduring as the land itself. Oh, she hated and loved in a breath! (S 98)

Neatly, the author catches her paradoxical intensity, and through it suggests to us today the secret of his enduring popular appeal.

SUGGESTIONS FOR READING

After a long period of scarcity, *A Scots Quair* is now available widely in collected form and in separate parts. In addition to the reprints of the one-volume Jarrolds edition, taken over and reprinted (and reset in part) by Hutchinson (used as the basis for discussion here) there are one-volume reprints of the *Quair* from Pan, and separate issues of each part, not always all in print. Schocken Books have a one-volume hardback of the *Quair* in the USA, and a paperback version from Pocket Books. In this country *Sunset Song* is available in a schools' edition in paperback from Longman with notes and introduction by the late J. T. Low (1971). Rare pre-war reprints of each novel from Jackdaw in paperback can still sometimes be found in second-hand bookshops. Verlag Volk and Welt in Berlin have three separate translations of each part of the *Quair*, published only in the DDR, translated by Hans Petersen with introductions by John Mitchell: they appeared as *Der Lange Weg durchs Ginstermoor* (1970), *Wolken über der Ebene* (1972) and *Flamme in grauem Granit* (1974). Other translations, notably in Czech, are all but unobtainable in this country.

Gibbon's primary claim to public notice, then, the *Quair*, is coming back into public hands, and with television popularity it seems set to give impetus to the work of evaluation. But his many other works prove more elusive. *Scottish Scene* was long scarce after its 1934 first publication, despite a brief (1974) re-issue by Chivers of Bath: the core essays and short stories by Gibbon were rescued by Ian Munro in *A Scots Hairst* (1967), and a slightly different selection published in paperback by D. M. Budge in *Smeddum: Stories and Essays* (1980) from Longman. *A Scots Hairst* includes fragments and school

essays, and portions of the material which formed the basis
for *The Speak of the Mearns* (1982) all of which has found its
way to the National Library of Scotland. It is a matter for
real regret that Gibbon did not live to work out this version
of his autobiography, the persona in a masculine form.

Chief in popularity among his other work was *Spartacus*,
long out of print till its 1970 reprint by Hutchinson: it is
now out of print once more. For the rest, Gibbon was a
real rarity in second-hand bookshops till the republication
in 1981 of *The Thirteenth Disciple* by Paul Harris of
Edinburgh, with an introduction by Douglas F. Young.
More republication is now under consideration, including
Gibbon's long-neglected science fiction. An interesting
development is the recent recording of cassette tape
commentaries (by Douglas F. Young) on *Sunset Song*, at
the instigation of the Association for Scottish Literary
Studies.

Criticism of Mitchell owes much to pioneer work by Ian
S. Munro whose friendship with the family, and access to
papers, led to the biography of 1966: the other ground-
breaking work was Douglas F. Young's *Beyond the Sunset*
(1973), the first complete critical discussion. Both books
are long out of print. The *Quair*, and Gibbon's fiction
generally, have naturally taken an important place in
wider discussions of Scottish literature, including Kurt
Wittig's *The Scottish Tradition in Literature* (1958/78) and
David Craig, *Scottish Literature and the Scottish People* (1961).
More recently, there have been substantial discussions in
Maurice Lindsay, *History of Scottish Literature* (1977), and
Francis Hart, *The Scottish Novel: A Critical Survey* (1978).
More recently still come two books, Alan Bold's *Modern
Scottish Literature* (1983) and Douglas Gifford's *Gunn and
Gibbon* (1983). Very recently there have appeared *Ten
Modern Scottish Novels* by Isobel Murray & Bob Tait
(1984), including an acute chapter on *A Scots Quair*, and
an excellent monograph *A Blasphemer & Reformer* (1984)
by William K. Malcolm; with new material available in

the libraries it seems inevitable that critical work will now appear in increasing quantity.

A steady stream of periodical articles continues to appear to indicate a continuing critical interest. W. R. Aitken has an invaluable checklist in *Scottish Literature in English and Scots* (1982), and there are checklists and updates in *The Bibliotheck*, the latest still in the press as these words are written. *A Companion to Scottish Culture* (1981) ed. David Daiches is a mine of information on the period and on associated topics, and a recent invaluable supplement is Trevor Royle's *Companion to Scottish Literature* (1983). Finally one should mention that there are annual surveys of work-in-progress and criticism in the supplements to *Scottish Literary Journal*, published by the Association for Scottish Literary Studies.

A sign of health in studies of Grassic Gibbon is the excellent recent work done on him at doctoral dissertation level, and two outstanding examples are theses by William Malcolm (Aberdeen, 1982) with a fine discussion of *Grey Granite*, and by M. J. McGrath (Edinburgh, 1983), with particular discussion of Gibbon's politics, a subject much generalised on but never before fully discussed.

An indication of the interest in Gibbon is the article criticism, much of it genuinely innovative. For instance Graham Trengove has a fascinating discussion of Gibbon's language, "Who is you? Grammar and Grassic Gibbon", *Scottish Literary Journal* 2, 2 (December, 1975), 47–62; Geoffrey Wagner, "The Greatest Since Galt: Lewis Grassic Gibbon", *Essays in Criticism* 2, 3 (July, 1952), 295–310; J. K. A. Thomaneck, "A Scots Quair in East Germany", *Scottish Literary Journal* 3, 1 (July, 1976), 62–6; D. M. Roskies, "Language, Class and Radical Perspective in A Scots Quair", *Zeitschrift für Anglistik und Amerikanistik* 29, 2 (1981), 142–53.

In late 1983 there are three interesting signs in Gibbon criticism. One is the impetus given to reading of the original texts by the showing of *Cloud Howe* and *Grey Granite* on television. One is the move to consider reprinting the texts. And one is the apparently unflagging interest in him at school level. While there is some danger that he may attract too much interest for his own good at that third level, the growing familiarity with the *Quair* must, we hope, make critical awareness a little closer.

Finally could be mentioned some work by the present writer on Gibbon in more specialised areas of discussion to complement this broader survey. There is relevant discussion in the closing essay in *Nineteenth Century Scottish Fiction: Critical Essays* ed. I. Campbell (1979), in *Kailyard: A New Assessment* (1981), and in the introduction and editorial matter to *The Speak of the Mearns* (1982). Articles are also relevant: see "George Douglas Brown's Kailyard Novel", *Studies in Scottish Literature* 12, 1 (July, 1974), 63–73; "The Science Fiction of John [*sic*] Leslie Mitchell", *Extrapolation* 16 (1974), 53–63; "Chris Caledonia: the Search for an Identity", *Scottish Literary Journal* 1, 2 (December, 1974), 45–57, and "James Leslie Mitchell's *Spartacus*: A Novel of Rebellion", *Scottish Literary Journal* 5, 1 (May, 1978), 53–60. Forthcoming are checklists of the surviving correspondence of James Leslie Mitchell in *The Bibliotheck* for 1984, and a paper on the abortive Festschrift project of 1935 in a future number of *Studies in Scottish Literature*.

August 1984.

INDEX